A WORLD BEYOND BELIEF:

Tales of a Real Estate Shaman

by G.W. Hardin

DreamSpeaker Creations, LLC
Denver, Colorado

Library of Congress Cataloging-in-Publication Data

Hardin, G.W.
A World Beyond Belief:
        Tales of a Real Estate Shaman
Autobiography, Real Estate, Inspiration, Spirituality

ISBN ... 978-1-893641-15-0
ISBN 10 ... 1893641155
1. Autobiography 2. Real Estate 3. Inspiration 4. Spiritualilty

Cover design and book design by G.W. Hardin

Set in 11 point Optima typeface

DEDICATED TO

Noah and Gabriel

Carriers of the Legacy of Love

ACKNOWLEDGMENT

To Sherif Sakr, who pressed me to write this book in spite of my protestations. To him goes my special gratitude for taking on the challenge of producer. Rarely can friendship and business mix successfully, but he pulled it off through his patience and wisdom.

Contents

Chapter 1

WHAT'S REAL? WHAT'S NOT?

At an early age, the strangest things terrified me. June bugs, for starters. It was as if I could hear their tiny voices as they ganged up on my window screen after everyone had gone to bed. Why they plucked the screen with their barbed legs during the hot summer nights mystified my child-mind. Why did they seek entrance into my bedroom when I wanted the exact opposite—to escape! Not until adulthood did I finally come to understand that human consciousness is the most miraculous—and the most limiting—creator of reality. The overarching question is, What holds rule over our lives? Are our self-created worlds real or figments?

Anyone in politics will tell you that fear is a potent weapon. But that weapon is like the proverbial sword—he who lives by it shall die by it. Humans are born with only two fears: fear of loud noises and fear of falling. Some psychology books add a third fear, that of sudden movement. All other fears are acquired or taught.

In Dr. Bruce Lipton's seminal work, *The Biology of Belief* (Hay House, 2011), he discovers that the overriding factors in determining who we are and who we become as human beings are belief systems. These guardians of figment are handed down to us and set in place by the time we are eight years old, when the subconscious anchors into place. The most disturbing finding in Lipton's work is the realization that the conscious mind is no match for the subconscious, which cannot be changed once it is set. In other words, Wordsworth's classic line, "The

Child is the Father of the man," is more than poetry. The remaining years of human life are determined by an eight-year-old living in our subconscious. That is unless we can replace the subconscious with systems that are not based upon belief but upon self-determination, oriented in oneness. Lipton suggests one method of replacing the subconscious but there are others. Later, I will describe the chief tool I use to help my clients replace their subconscious belief systems that imprison them—cursing them with judgment over what's real and what's not.

As an adult, I eventually realized that the June bugs were symbolic of my own belief system that the world around me loomed as a terrifying and violent place bent on vanquishing anyone or anything threatening its ways. It wasn't until I was an adult that I discovered that my own personal power, my own innate giftedness, threatened others who could not or would not believe in themselves. And rather than lift themselves up out of their self-made gutters, they chose to tear others down, in hopes that their gutters would be filled with company.

One of the most devastating acquired fears is the fear of being alone, abandoned, marooned to an island called the Self, where we can never be good enough because we believe it to be so. When I comprehended the main reason for my own self-condemnation had sprung from repeated condemnation by grownups who could not trust in themselves, who continually marginalized anyone who did not fit into their belief systems, who ignorantly transformed walls of protection into self-made prisons, I rapidly began to suspect anything that was called "real."

"Real," for me, came to a crashing death in 1968. At the time I had been stationed at the National Security Agency (NSA), a mere sergeant in the Air Force. Fort Meade, Maryland, served as the home of NSA, the most secret organization in the world, affectionately known as the "Puzzle Palace," named aptly for its ability to break just about any encryption device on the planet. My job was to report Romanian Intelligence, having been well trained as a linguist. After a year of sheer boredom (the joke around the Puzzle Palace was that Romania didn't reveal enough intelligence to fly a Piper Cub), activity around Romania's borders changed rapidly.

World forces moved into battle as the Soviet Union bulldozed its way into what was then called Czechoslovakia. Czech president Alexandr Dubcek had instigated reforms that threatened the very foundation of Communism in his country. The Russian Communist Party was already having fits with Tito in Yugoslavia and Ceausescu in Romania. Unable to tolerate yet a third country's rumblings within world Communism, Soviet Russia invaded.

Finding Czechoslovakia easy pickings, Soviet Russia's lustful eyes roamed in the direction of nearby Romania. Why not get rid of Ceausescu while they were at it? That put me in the front row observing what many considered the inevitable. Tanks and armies began to amass on the northern borders of Romania, which turned my boring workstation into Command Central.

Not only were Soviet armies on the move, so were NATO ships and Romanian Civil Defense forces. I sat at my station watching the world become a chess match as global history moved dynamically before me. While monitoring traffic one day, I felt my headphones yanked off from behind. Turning around to chew out the culprit, I froze in place counting the number of bigwigs flanking my station. One officer, with enough silver on his shoulders to create an eight-piece place setting, held a memorandum in his hand.

"Sergeant, this is from the President," he announced in a rather ominous tone. "The Russians are about to invade Romania. The President wants to know if the Romanian Army and Civil Defense can hold the Soviet Army off for twenty-four hours. The President is making a decision whether to aid Romania by dropping in an airborne division. He wants an answer in fifteen minutes. Get any and all the information you need. Here is the latest intelligence we have smuggled out of Romania. Translate what you can and give us an answer."

My first thought was, *OK, who put you up to this?* My best friend, a Russian translator, was notorious for his practical jokes to pass the boredom. I kept looking to see where he might be hiding. But all I saw was a half-dozen serious faces staring at me.

"Fifteen minutes," repeated the officer sternly.

"Yes, sir," I replied, recognizing there was no prank behind the situation. I snapped into action as I pressed my earphones against my ears, getting the intelligence ready for rapid examination. My mind began to buzz from the adrenaline, which caused me to start laughing. Immediately, I caught myself and held my breath. This kind of laughter was how I handled extreme stress, an old habit I had never been able to break, which had gotten me into serious trouble in the past.

As the voices in my earphones rattled on, I realized that what I was listening to was the same old information I had been listening to ever since Czechoslovakia's invasion. Rather than turn around and tell the bigwigs what I knew, I decided to take up the entire fifteen minutes because my mind was starting to comprehend that I was being asked whether World War III was about to begin.

President Johnson had already announced four months earlier that he would not seek re-election. The Vietnam War had gone badly for him, and he had taken a beating in the polls. The country was tearing itself apart with war protests, the likes of which the United States had never seen. Johnson had nothing to lose and everything to gain as a footnote in history. It occurred to me that he was betting the farm on what I would say in the next five minutes. Extreme emotion began to numb my body, almost to the point of paralysis. I already knew the answer to the question the President had asked. Hell, I had known the answer for two days. What kept me from saying anything was the stunning realization that what would pass my lips could very well bring us into World War III. What would it mean if I were wrong? What if I were missing some important factoid? Could the wrong interpretation bring devastating consequences to the world? I almost started laughing again.

Then the absurdity of the entire situation struck me, clearing my mind. This struggle between world powers was complete nonsense. Nobody was really in charge. Men who called themselves leaders were relying on nobodies like me to tell them how to play their chess game. Shouldn't someone just tell them to stop playing the stupid game? To me, the answer was an obvious Yes! But I also knew that these boys in men's bodies had reached their places of power because they had surrounded themselves with power brokers who refused to tell the king what the king *ought* to do rather than tell the king what the king *can* do. This was history repeating itself. Instead of Thomas Becket and King Henry, it was me and President Johnson. And I was definitely no Thomas

Becket holding Archbishop of Canterbury status. Three stripes rested on my sleeves. Either I answered the king's question as to what he *could* do, or they'd replace me with someone who would. There was no way to tell the king what he *ought* to do: Stop playing the game.

This had not been the only time "Landslide Lyndon" had put the world on the edge of World War III. Johnson loved to create illusion. His entire political career had hinged on his extraordinary ability to bluff. His nickname stood as a testimonial to his first elected position where he made it look like he had won a landslide victory when in actuality he had barely even won, and then only by vote tampering. Almost no one knows of his taking the United States to DEFCON 1 (imminent war status) over the USS *Pueblo* incident with North Korea. From my workstation, I had also witnessed his order sending the U.S. fleet toward the Korean Peninsula, rattling sabers with China. China made sure he backed down.

Slowly I removed my headphones. Nausea began spreading across my abdomen as I turned to those who wielded power. They stood as if made of stone. Not a muscle moved on their faces as I began to speak.

"Sir," I almost yelled, trying to get past the lump in my throat. "Romania has mined all the bridges the Soviets need to cross. They have already called up the Civil Defense. That means every man who can walk has enlisted. They are ready. The Russians are probably aware of this mobilization as well."

"Are you sure, Sergeant?"

I wanted to tell him that the only thing I was sure of was how lunatic the entire scenario appeared. But instead I said, "Sir, the Romanians knew two days ago that the Russians would not stop at Czechoslovakia. They can hold the Russians for twenty-four hours."

With that, the entire flank of bigwigs turned and marched out. Once I made it home, I kept vomiting.

As the days passed, I watched how the chess match played out. The Russians weren't in the mood for World War III. All I could think about for days was how insane the world of politics actually is. At this young age of twenty-one I came to realize that what we call real is nothing but illusion. The world stage was just that: a stage. Players played their make-believe parts created by men who did not know themselves or their own personal boundaries, and thus could not respect the boundaries of others. Their two-edged swords of fear are thought to be their weapon of control. But in truth, that sword cuts both ways: indeed, in the end, they will destroy themselves. From that day forward I never believed "real" again—of any kind.

BEYOND BELIEF: FAITH OR TRUST?

In my decades of working with clients, I have accumulated some of the most unbelievable stories you'll ever hear. At one time, these tales were just too impossible for people to comprehend. But no longer. The world of quantum physics has become the new spirituality, the new horizon of a truth that cannot be contained or limited. Not only can people now handle the impossible (because science is no longer the citadel of the certain and the undeniable), but it's time for the impossible to open the gateways into an unlimited possible.

I am a scientist. I worked hard to get my bachelor of science degree in mathematics, and even harder to pursue my master of science in biostatistics, which I walked away from. The last step toward writing my thesis ended up being my last step in academia. Like our National Security Agency, academia is invested in control of knowledge—the fashioning of illusion. Most people think mathematics is a "pure" science. "Numbers don't lie," we are told. To the contrary, put in the hands of illusionists, numbers can be manipulated to say whatever their handlers wish them to say. That's what caused me to leave academia. Like the illusion of world power, "science" rises or falls on what people choose to believe.

The bastion of Science, however, has been turned on its ear. Quantum mechanics has replaced the Newtonian laws that once ruled the universe. Heisenberg uncertainty and quantum potentials have now solidly established that anything is possible. I can now welcome you to my world.

To enter the world I have uncovered, we must start with a language we agree on. Paradoxically, words are powerful tools, and yet profoundly limiting. As an author and lecturer, I constantly have to meet people where they are if they are ever going to be able to hear what I have to say. If I speak Swahili and you speak German, then we have little chance to communicate well with one another. So a decision has to be made. Do I ask you to learn Swahili or is it incumbent upon me to learn German? It's my experience that I have to come to where you are if I wish you to hear me. If I am going to be of assistance to you, I must learn German.

I believe Bruce Lipton's work has shown that the basics of biology, or existence, depends on perception. And in the process of studying perception, Lipton has unveiled what I call one of the veils of forgetfulness: belief systems.

In the collection of the Nag Hammadi gnostic texts dwells a manuscript, one of my favorite of all time: "The Apocryphon of John." The writer tells of a being called the "Archon," the word being Greek for "ruler" or "lord." In our current mythology, we might see the Archon as the embodiment of evil or darkness. The story goes that when Wisdom witnessed the creation of Man, she left with Man a heritage that shone far more grand than the rest of creation. Seeing this, the Archon decided to create the five veils of forgetfulness so that humanity will not be able to see its own glory, its own wonder. It is only now that humanity is in the middle of casting off the veils of forgetfulness. And greatest among the veils are belief systems as described by Dr. Lipton.

At the core of what I have discovered is the notion of knowing self, as well as the Self. For too long I uttered the adage, "Believe in yourself." But what does that actually mean? As Lipton reveals, all beliefs come from a source outside of self, trying to influence the consciousness and subconsciousness of the self. Thus there is an implied contradiction in issuing an imperative statement regarding self based upon a source outside of self.

The next imperative I gave up was "Have faith in yourself," or more simply, "Have faith." This adage gets a bit more tricky because oftentimes people equate faith with trust. In those instances, I leave the semantics alone and move on. But how often do people recognize that "faith," like belief, comes from outside of oneself. Even if one wishes to take the notion of faith to a beatific level, most masters teach that the best place to find the Divine is within oneself. From a quantum point of view that means we are a part of the whole—there are many gifts but one Spirit; there are many parts but one body.

That leads me to the three rules for finding happiness or success: (1) trust yourself, (2) trust yourself, and (3) trust yourself. The best way to establish trust in oneself is to "know thyself" (Socrates).

Please keep this in mind as you travel with me on a journey that is impossibly possible. And when we are done, you will find we have taken the alchemist's path, which means we should end up right where we began—with the fullness of Self. That which is full and complete. Or as the angels like to say, "You are perfect, whole, and complete, just the way you are." The real trick is finding out who you are.

Chapter 2

The Swami and the Ghost

"There's no such thing as ghosts." How many times had I heard that as a child? Yet how many times had friends flocked to horror movies to be scared out of their skins by ghosts who preyed upon the unsuspecting? Admit it. People like to be scared. Why is that?

One of the oldest documented fears is xenophobia, fear of the unknown. Society has determined that our best interests are served by staying at arm's length from that which we do not comprehend. Culturally, we have been taught to avoid anything that could potentially harm us. So parents warn their children incessantly in the name of safety. Understandable. Yet as these same children grow into adulthood, they love to dare themselves with fright. They derive a pleasure from realizing that they can and do, survive the unknown.

A recent study conducted by Eduardo Andrade (University of Berkeley) and Joel Cohen (University of Florida) argues that past theories as to why people like to be scared may be erroneous. They posit, "The assumption of people's inability to experience positive and negative affect at the same time is incorrect." [1] In other words, we love to find out we can survive at the same time we feel danger or fear. It's a rush.

The study hints at a greater truth when it comes to human consciousness. In the world of physics, it was thought at one time that there were two states of existence: waves and particles. Period. That stood as the makeup of the universe. But quantum physics later shook the scientific community with the discovery of a third state. In this third state—which should be impossible—a particle and a wave exist simultaneously. This discovery took on various names, but today this third quantum state is called "the point of choosing." What experiments in quantum labs have shown is that consciousness determines whether this third quantum state will act as a particle or a wave.

Andrade and Cohen imply that a similar truth applies around being scared: A person can experience both fear and pleasure at the same time from the same event. As in quantum physics, we are at a point of choosing. We can decide whether to hold onto a learned fear or let go of the fear only to realize that there actually is nothing to be scared of in the first place. When this happens, the power of the fear starts to dissipate, if not disappear. In truth, it's up to us whether we choose to be afraid or not. And that choice ultimately is based upon our awareness of ourselves.

So when a soon-to-be client called me about a haunting in her house, I had to revisit my entire upbringing around the topic of ghosts. Do they exist? Intellectually, I had read several books on the subject of spirits. What I came to terms with was the notion that there are as many levels of spiritual forces as there are levels within corporations. The level that I had been called to address is what the professionals call a "disembodied spirit" or a "discorporate spirit." For some reason, this spirit had shown up in ordinary reality. And to make matters even more interesting, the ghost had been spotted by a notable, if not famous, swami who was visiting Fort Collins, Colorado, and staying at my client's house. The Indian community of Fort Collins called him Swami

---

[1] "On the Consumption of Negative Feelings," *Journal of Consumer Research*: August 2007.

Ji. I had read a lot about swamis but had never met one. The more I heard, the more my curiosity grew.

THE STORY BEHIND NISHA

Nisha Sapru (not her real name) had lived in Fort Collins for years, a recognized intellectual from a respected family in India. She also stood out as a spiritual leader, thus the reason for her sponsoring and housing Swami Ji. After his first night staying in Ms. Sapru's house, he calmly and matter-of-factly responded to the question of how he had slept. While sipping his Starbucks latte, one of his favorite luxuries while visiting America, he reported that he had experienced a fitful night because of the ghost that kept visiting his room.

"Ghost?" said Ms. Sapru. "There's a ghost in my house?"

"Yes," replied Swami Ji, "but he is not a bad ghost. He is just troubled. I would be most grateful if you brought somebody in to remove it. It really shouldn't be here. His work here is done. He should be moving on."

"How did he get here?" she asked. "I wasn't aware my house was haunted."

"I don't know," answered Swami Ji truthfully. "There is some kind of disturbance that allows him to be here. I am not experienced with such matters. It's best to bring in someone who knows about these things."

That's when I got the phone call from Ms. Sapru. My reputation had nothing to do with ghostbusting. However, I was known for my dealing with unexplainable phenomena, which I will get into later.

"G.W., my name is Nisha Sapru, and I've been calling every-where to get help with a situation that has occurred at my home. And your name keeps coming up." The distressed woman spoke with the most beautiful Indian accent. A grin crept across my face at the thought that my reputation had spread. However, I came to find out that Nisha did not want to sell her house nor was she interested in buying a new one. So I asked for more detail as to why my name came up and what it was she wished from me.

For six months prior, I had been working with real estate agents in the Fort Collins area who needed help with houses that would not sell. But my foray into real estate had actually begun two years earlier in Denver when a friend of mine had invited me out to dinner. While enjoying the food and wine, I took notice of his somewhat melancholy mood. Pressed for details, he confessed his difficulty with selling two of his commercial real estate investments. The buildings had sat empty going on the second year and he was now hemorrhaging money from the deal. When I enquired about their history, I found out why my buddy had come to purchase the buildings at bargain prices. They had been part of a large nightclub that authorities had closed down upon discovering that drugs were being sold out of them. That gave me an idea.

"You know about feng shui, right?" I asked him. He informed me that he had, in fact, hired a feng shui master in the past to clear his own house. After he and his lover had broken up, the house was in emotional turmoil—gadgets kept breaking and problems kept showing up around the house. So at the urging of friends, he had the feng shui master clear the dwelling, and the disruptions ceased. The ancient Chinese practice was a mystery to most Westerners, but as long as it worked, that's all he cared about.

"Well, there is a reason why feng shui works," I said. "I look at it as nature-based quantum entanglement. From a scientific point of view, everything is connected. There is a famous theorem in quantum mechanics called Bell's Theorem. Simply stated, Bell's Theorem proves that all of life is one. No matter how far apart any two objects are, they still are connected at some level. I believe feng shui is a testimonial to human consciousness connecting anything and everything. If a human being wishes to use his awareness to bring two completely unrelated objects into his field of recognition or observation, those two objects become quantumly entangled. If you like, I can show you."

"Are you kidding?" my friend exclaimed. "Of course I want to see! If this is related to why my properties aren't selling, I want to know about it."

Looking around to make sure we weren't being watched, I asked him to put either one of his arms straight out in front of himself. "OK, now I want you to show your strength as I try to push your arm down. Move it a little more to the side so I don't hit the table."

"You aren't going to hit the table," he smirked. "I think you know my own strength."

"Humor me," I smiled. As he moved his arm to a safer position, I tried to push his arm down. Rigid. It wouldn't move. It was obvious the guy worked out.

"Ha!" he laughed. "Told you so."

"Not so fast," I said. "Watch this. All I'm going to do is take my empty wine glass and tip it against this bud vase. Like so." Carefully I leaned the glass snugly against the ripples in the bud base. "OK. You see the tipped wine glass. It's just a wine glass, right? Well, let me test the strength of your arm again."

"OK," my buddy said as he offered his arm once again. With little force, I pushed his arm down to his leg. The look on his face was that of a man who had just been cheated. "Do that again," he demanded. This time his arm proved even weaker. "How did you do that?"

"Now wait," I said. "I'm not done yet." I carefully reset the wine glass to its normal upright position. "Let me test your strength again."

Once again he stuck his arm out, but this time it was strongly rigid like before. "What the hell," he gasped. "What's going on here?"

"Let me do this one more time to make sure you register with what's happening." Once again I leaned the wine glass against the bud vase, and once again his arm went fully weak. The grin on his face said it all.

At about that time, the waiter had quietly arrived at our table, noticing the wine glass. He cleared his throat as he picked up the glass, probably wondering if I was trying to get his attention. "More wine?" he asked, holding the glass politely.

"It's on me," chirped my friend. "Waiter, please bring him a glass of pinot noir. It's his favorite."

"Certainly," said the waiter, bowing as he left.

"Well," I said, "let's not waste the moment. Since the waiter showed up to put everything in order, we should test your arm one more time." And once again, the arm showed full strength.

"You've got my attention," my friend said. "What does this have to do with my unsold buildings?"

"The point I'm trying to make is that there may be forces associated with the building that have everything out of balance. Feng shui is only one of the forces of nature that can determine harmony or balance. There's also geomagnetic forces and karmic forces among others. You should have me come over and check your buildings out. I'd like to help. You do so much for me."

A few days later my buddy was unlocking the first of the empty buildings and showing me his bargain. As we examined the various sections, we came to an area that seemed unusually cold to me. "Can we stop here a bit?" I asked. Carefully, I pulled out two dowsing rods from my briefcase, and began checking the space.

A curious look wrinkled his face. "What are those?"

"Oh, you haven't heard of dowsing rods?"

"You mean, like water witching?"

"Yeah, that was one of its earlier names. There are others."

"So why are you looking for water?"

"Water isn't the only thing these little guys can find. I haven't told you this before, but I have a gift. It's called 'geomancy.' Geomancy is what birds use to follow their migration paths. Those migration paths actually are created by what are called 'ley lines,' which are geo-magnetic eddies or climes created by the Earth's magnetic field. Think of it like watching the surface of a bay. Sometimes you'll notice different coloring patterns in the water created by differences in temperature or differences in currents. Large ships create their own climes in a bay with their large propellers that stir up the water and leave recognizable patterns in their wake. Sometimes these patterns will remain for a couple days. In World War II, these patterns were used by ship hunters to track battleships. This was one of the methods used by the British against the German battleship, the *Bismarck*, which they had long pursued and finally sunk.

"I am like migrating birds, in that I have these mineral deposits in my brain, called magnetite, that allow me to pick up on any abnormalities in the magnetic field. One day, as part of a tour, I walked into a generator room of the Dalles Dam on the Columbia River, and nearly passed out. The tour guides had to escort me off the dam. That's when I began to realize that I was different from others.

"What I've picked up here is an aberration in the building. If I focus on this long enough, I can figure out what's causing it. But I use dowsing rods to speed things up. A master dowser out of Montana named Michael Hoefler taught me how to use these puppies."

Michael had also taught me how to make my own dowsing rods, which I did, finding that my homemade version worked much better for me than anything I had used previously. Its makeup was simple. I bought a three-foot bronze welding rod at Ace Hardware, cut it in half, and then bent the halves about a third of the way down at ninety degrees, thus creating a handle five inches in length and a horizontal thirteen inches in length. By wrapping silver wire along the horizontal of each rod, I found it worked amazingly well for me.

My friend stared blankly at me as I began walking back and forth across the path of climes I had detected. At certain points the dowsing rods would swing wildly outward in my hands, while in other spots they would swiftly swing inward almost touching one another. After several passes back and forth, I found myself facing a wall.

"What's behind this wall?" I asked.

"That's the garage," my friend answered, a thousand questions flooding his mind. "What's going on? What are you doing? Why the weaving back and forth?"

"Sorry, usually I'm more considerate in telling clients what I'm doing. I just don't think of you as a client. There's a strong abnormality in this part of the building. It's being caused by something behind this wall. The energy in here is really bad, highly negative. People subconsciously pick up on stuff like this. Kind of like how you feel when an architectural design is working or not. Can we get into the garage so I can check out what's causing this?"

"Sure," he said. "Follow me." After leading me through a maze of hallways, he opened a steel door and turned on a set of lights. There in the garage was a sixteen-foot-high wall painted with psychedelic patterns worthy of a madman. I walked over to the wild design with dowsing rods in hand. They went crazy. No matter which angle or what direction I walked, they constantly pointed at the twelve-foot-high pattern of electric green and yellow.

Whoever created this must have been on acid, was my initial reaction as I stared up at the zigzags and pyramidal shapes formed in a large circular mosaic of interlocking geometric patterns. "This is it," I concluded.

"What's it?" my friend asked.

"This is what is causing all the negative energy in the complex."

"How?"

"How long has this been here?" I asked, ignoring his question for the moment.

"Ever since I bought the building. Since it was in the garage, I decided not to remove it. Kinda sixties-like. Quirky. Added a little personality to the dungeonlike darkness of the garage."

"Well, whoever painted this was on drugs. And they knew what they were doing. In ancient times, magicians or black witches would use what are called 'sigils' to create portals, or dimensional openings. They would then invite spirits into ordinary reality through these portals. In some cases, evil would be the end result of bargaining with these beings of consciousness. Whoever painted this created a portal. And they used sigils that few people are aware of. You have to remove this design."

My buddy looked at me as if he had just finished watching the movie *The Exorcist*. "What? Are you serious? It's just paint. And that's a cinderblock wall. Do you know how much it would cost me to scrub that spray paint off?"

"Didn't I lead you to this spot without knowing it was here? I'm telling you this portal has got to be closed. And the best way to close it is to remove the sigils. If you can't scrape it off, then paint over it. But use a dark paint so that any vibration is absorbed. If you want to sell this building, you'll cover this up."

Within two days my buddy had coated the twelve-foot-high spray-paint mandala with heavy black paint. Within a month a buyer showed up for the building. Word spread after that. My friend had informed commercial real estate friends of his in the Denver area of what I was able to do. Within a year I was working with seven different real estate agents.

My phone conversation with Ms. Sapru reminded me of this first real estate encounter with my past friend. Once again I was about to enter new territory, and it intrigued me. Her voice, on the other hand, reflected a fear of the unknown. That should have tipped me off right away. Even though her Hindu upbringing was based on solid familiarity with the spiritual, hearing that her house was haunted, to her utter oblivion, shook her. It was as if some kind of shame burdened her. Personally, I felt that the entire episode was kinda cool. But I gave up paying attention to what societal norms dictate long ago. If the swami felt comfortable enough announcing the haunting, shouldn't his followers feel comfortable as well?

Nisha's questions were many, and I felt it was my job to inform and educate on matters that few ever discuss. The universe is changed one person at a time. Even though I had no experience in dealing with ghosts, she felt my reputation in dealing with the unexplainable stood out against amateur ghostbusters who lacked any serious credentials. Her background as an academic lent her to taking seriously my professional, yet otherworldly, adventures in real estate. Her and Swami Ji's reputations had to be taken into consideration, knowing full well that the outcome of this bizarre undertaking would most likely spread like wildfire among the Indian community. The next day I arrived on her doorstep.

"Thank you for coming right away," effused Nisha. "Swami had another unsettling night, and I feel terrible that this has happened. Who knew? How does anyone know when a ghost is in their house?"

I had no answer for her. Rather than get into explanations I didn't have, I informed Nisha that I'd like to check out the outside of the house before we went inside.

"The outside?" A puzzled look flashed back at me. "The ghost is inside."

"I understand. But I've learned, when it comes to real estate, to inspect the environment surrounding unexplainable situations. Sometimes geomagnetic phenomena are used to feed the energy of paranormal events within a house. Sometimes the land has a karma that must be addressed, especially in Colorado. In fact, Fort Collins has a reputation for what is called the 'curse of the Horsetooth shaman.' During what was called the 'Colorado Wars,' the legend goes that a powerful and greatly respected shaman climbed to the holy ground on Horsetooth Mountain, just above what was then called Camp Collins, and placed a curse on the land occupied by white men. I pay attention to accounts like this even though I've never been able to corroborate any facts around this particular curse.

"Another area I like to explore is bad feng shui, even though I'm not a feng shui master. I use my dowsing rods to find any anomalies on the land." I pulled my dowsing rods out of my satchel and showed them to her. "Will it be OK to use these? Your neighbors might see me outside. I wish to show respect to your guest as well. Are there any Indian customs I should pay attention to?"

Nisha smiled as I showed her the dowsing rods. I wasn't sure whether this was a good or bad sign. "Please, use whatever you need. Swami Ji respects all beliefs, as do I. Is it all right if I accompany you? Are you OK with my asking questions?"

"Yes, and yes. I think I'll just walk around the property and see what I can pick up in my body first." As I walked around the grounds, Nisha shadowed me quietly. As I meandered behind the northeast corner of the house, a tingling spread across my back. I stopped suddenly with Nisha nearly bumping into me.

"So sorry," she said, growing curious as to why I had frozen in place.

Backing up about ten feet, I once again traversed the corner, and again felt the disturbance. Time to find out the source. The rods crossed as I approached a certain section of the corner. Focusing my eyes on the ground, I began to scan the area. What I discovered was a copper rod that had been pounded into the ground with about three inches of the rod showing above ground.

"Has this always been here?" I asked.

She approached to see what I was pointing at. "Oh. That. No. That's a copper thing placed there by a feng shui master I paid to check out my house years ago. She said this area was imbalanced and needed metal."

That was the clue I needed. I began formulating questions in my head, directing my higher consciousness to answer through the dowsing rods. *Is there an imbalance of feng shui around this copper rod?* I asked. The rods stood motionless in my hands, which for me meant the answer to be No. *Did there used to be an imbalance in this area?* The tips of the rods swung inward, which meant Yes. *Is this area of the house related to the appearance of the ghost?* The rods swung in once again. *Is there a geomagnetic anomaly that's causing this?* The answer was Yes once again.

I define geomagnetic anomalies as any abnormal interaction involving the Earth's magnetic field. These can involve ley lines, Hartmann lines, Curry lines, dragon lines, portals, vortexes, gateways, or wormholes, all of which I will explain later.

Can I, may I, should I examine this anomaly? As the rods swung inward, I began to formulate in my mind what might be affecting the house that the feng shui master had picked up on. I make it a practice to ask permission when I am considering bringing forth information that may have an effect on what we call ordinary reality. Likewise, I check before I make any changes to make sure I am honoring Mother Earth and the people I have been hired to serve. Nisha had already brought in a feng shui master to instill balance to her house. The last thing I needed to do was to disturb that balance. Past experience told me I need to tread carefully. However, something was occurring that had allowed this ghost to show up. At least according to Swami Ji. I had not yet seen any indications of a ghost. After running through possible causes that might allow the ghost the energy it needed to appear, I decided to check for a ley line.

After a few minutes of meandering back and forth, having set the intention of finding a ley line, the rods suddenly crossed. "Aha," I said, delighted my intuition had proven correct.

"What?" asked Nisha. "What's going on?"

"Give me a few more minutes and I'll explain." What I was looking for was the path of the ley line. If the ley line were intersecting the house, it might explain the source of energy used by the ghost. Any spirit interacting with third-dimensional reality needs energy just the same as we do in occupying our bodies. Just because you don't have a body doesn't relieve you from the need for life force or energy. This supposition was proving true in this case.

As I checked several other possible paths farther away from the corner of the house, I ran across the ley line once again. By using the two points my dowsing rods had indicated, I could now draw a straight line. And that straight line went right through the basement of the house. This was my first clue.

"Nisha, there is a ley line that crosses your property, and it goes right through your basement." I straightened my arm to show her the path I had found.

"Oh, my," she whispered. "That's where Swami's bedroom is. What do we do now?"

"Let's go inside so I can check out the rest of the house, especially the basement."

Nisha quickly ushered me through the back door into the kitchen. Immediately she wanted to host me with fresh fruit and tea. Even after I told her I was fine, she insisted I sit for a bit while she nourished me. I had met Jewish mothers who insisted on good hostessing and I had met Italian mothers who insisted on good eating, but this was new to me. I would find out later that Indian mothers carry a rich tradition of the Divine Mother, and often lavish their guests with fine food and delicious teas. This new adventure was proving to be quite fun.

Nisha wanted to know more about me. I, in turn, sought out information about her house and her family. History can sometimes be quite important in finding the source of unexplainable problems. Nisha had a wonderful family, a grown son, a daughter about to go off to college, and a brilliant husband who worked in the high-tech industry. To listen to Nisha, I might as well have been listening to an episode of *Leave It to Beaver*. For those of you too young to remember, the Cleaver family, including Beaver, was the ideal TV family, historically located somewhere between *The Adventures of Ozzie and Harriet* (the Nelsons) and *The Partridge Family*.

A part of me wondered if Nisha was actually trying to avoid the inevitable: meeting up with the ghost. Any mention of the ghost seemed to put her on edge. As an American, Nisha had been subjected to the same TV horror as the rest of us. Her kids were like other American kids, insisting they be allowed to go to the movies and watch videos with their friends, which included a diet ranging from *Nightmare on Elm Street* to *Poltergeist* to *The Blair Witch Project*. Like it or not, I was here to find a ghost and get rid of it. Any fear on Nisha's part only added to the problem. However, I began to sense that something in the family might be contributing to the appearance of the unwelcome spirit.

After checking out the rest of the house, I finally ended up in the basement—alone. Nisha decided she'd hang out in the living room. I couldn't blame her. I, myself, had no idea what I might encounter. Right away my dowsing rods started swinging outward, giving me the signal of No, no, no. I wasn't sure whether that was a signal for me to get out of the basement or the ghost asking me not to proceed. As the rods continued to swing outward, I found myself unable to get any more answers.

In order to continue, I had to clear the rods. Taking a deep breath, I spun the rods in my hands yelling out the words, "Clear, clear." After balancing the rods in my hands once again, I commanded, "Give me a yes." When the rods swung inward, I presumed I had control of them again. I now knew that the ghost was present. The air around me began to cool. I dismissed the sensation as the coolness of the basement. But the hair on my arms began to rise. That had never happened before. Silently, I asked my angels to assist me.

Nisha had told me which bedroom was Swami's. I was headed there when the rods went out of control. In his room, the smell of incense still lingered in the air. I didn't know about ghosts, but I did know that certain incense could be used to clear a space of negativity. Some believe it can also clear away any evil spirits. At this point, it occurred to me that I ought to find out what kind of ghost I was confronting. The swami had indicated that he found the ghost merely troubling. However, I needed to determine what its overall role was in order to best address the situation. If its purpose was evil, then I would have to take precautions to protect myself. However, I knew I had to stay away from fear. Many entities that invade from other dimensions use fear as a source of sustenance. In the worst cases, fear is like candy to these beings. You will see details of such in another case history later.

Once again I asked the question, Can I? May I? Should I?—directing my enquiry at acquiring information about the ghost. The rods swung inward.

Yes.

"Is there a ghost right now in the basement area?"

Yes, said the rods. I decided to ask again, just to make sure—this time being even more careful to make sure my ego was out of the way. The answer was still Yes.

"Is it evil in nature?"

No.

"Is it in the highest good of those living here that it be removed?"

Yes.

"What allows it to be here? Psychic energy?"

No.

"Karma?"

The right rod swung inward while the left rod stayed still. For me, this was an indicator that the question either had to be reworded (because a yes or a no would be a misguiding answer) or the answer was a maybe. I decided to reword the question.

"Is it attracted to the karma of someone in the house?"

Yes.

"Can I, may I, should I find out who that is right now?"

No. I am usually surprised when I get a no like this. It means that people are involved who are not ready to face the facts of what is going on or lessons are being taught and my bringing in new information would interfere with those lessons.

"May I speak with the ghost?"

Yes.

My gift is not clairvoyance nor clairaudience. I'm a geomancer. Normally I don't physically see or hear angels or masters. I'm more clairsentient, which means I feel them first. Once I operate on that level, I sometimes am able to see an angel or master holographically, not unlike the holographs generated by R2D2 in *Star Wars.* On occasion, that leads me to actually hearing them. For me to be able to have that with this ghost, I first had to find out where it was hiding. I asked, "Is the ghost in this room?"

No.

So the hunt began. Besides the main rec room, there were three other rooms in the basement. After deftly using the dowsing rods to track energy and life force, rather than the ghost itself, I found the ghost hanging out in the rec room, next to the fireplace. I noted that this was no ordinary fireplace. It stood out for two reasons. Being made out of Colorado red rock meant it was iron rich. The rock also sparkled brightly from the light entering the basement window, which meant the makeup was rich in crystal content (not unusual for Colorado rock).

My strategy was to find out two factors that would allow me to remove the ghost: (1) Why was it here? and (2) What was its source of energy that allowed it to operate in ordinary reality? By carefully wording my questions, a pattern of information wove a tapestry that showed that the ghost was the spirit of an older man who used pity to get attention and to attract company—not unlike the old adage, "Misery loves company." I tend to call such people "emotional vampires." Because of my efforts to dig up information, other aspects of the ghost came into focus. An outline of his face began to take on detail. A scruffy beard faded in with shape and color. As the connection grew stronger, I picked up on the thoughts of the materializing consciousness. An overbearing sense of pity grew around me.

One factor became apparent. This being was not malevolent. There would be no need for protection or confrontation. I discovered that the old man had led a life of loneliness caused by constantly pushing people away with his complaining and whining about troubles. This man had become so attached (some would say addicted) to pity, that at the time of death, his spirit refused to cross over to the supernal world, unable to face the consequences of the life it had led—or more accurately, the life it had *not* led. Instead, it lingered in and around ordinary reality, now preying on people who fostered the same kind of energy the old man used to use when he was alive. What that told me was that I would later have to discover who in the family was "feeding" this ghost. I might then be able to encourage this family member to learn from the ghost and live a life not dependent on pity.

My next step was to find out how the ghost was getting the energy it needed to come and go. The evidence indicated that it was not a permanent resident. After checking the space around the fireplace, I found what I call a portal. Later I will describe the different kinds of portals and how they function. The point was that the ghost was using the portal as a doorway, and that somehow had to be stopped. My first question was whether the best interest of the family and the land would be served by closing the portal.

No.

That left me only two options: (1) either place some kind of guardian, like an angel, at the opening or (2) change the vibration of the portal so low vibrational beings such as the ghost could not come through. The rods indicated all would best be served by changing the vibration. There are four ways I use to change the vibrations of a space: sound, sacred oils or smudging, color or light, or crystals.

Colorado is blessed with lots of rose quartz. When called into situations having to deal with real estate, I normally have a bag of rose quartz or amethyst as part of my tool kit. Not knowing any better, I labeled this situation to be a real estate matter, so I had rose quartz with me. After blessing two of the crystals, I placed them on either side of the fireplace with the intent that only beings of high vibration, anchored in love, would be allowed to pass through.

My next step was to call in one of my angels to escort the disturbed spirit into the light now surrounding the portal. The spirit would then finally meet and engage with what psychologist Michael Newton, PhD, calls its "soul council." In Newton's books, *Journey of Souls* (Llewellyn Publications, 1994) and *Destiny of Souls* (Llewellyn Publications, 2000), he gives detailed information on how souls operate in and out of ordinary reality. After death, most souls move to the spirit world where they initially meet loved ones. Afterward they come before their soul council, a circle of advanced souls heaped in wisdom and love. It is the duty of the soul council to have the returned soul review its life in the physical world so as to learn more in its continued journey we call life.

I asked my angel, Bahram, whom I like to use in situations like this, to escort the wandering soul to the spirit realm. As I watched, I saw the old man immediately try to use pity to justify remaining in ordinary reality. The angel lovingly insisted that the spirit would be better served by moving on with its journey toward growth and enlightenment. As I witnessed the energy in the room shift and the hologram disappear, I checked with my dowsing rods to make sure the old man was gone for good.

Yes.

I then had to make sure that no other unwelcome visitors would be able to move through the portal.

No, they wouldn't.

Two days later Nisha called me again. Swami Ji was delighted. He had slept soundly for two nights in a row, and now wished to meet me. Could I come over and spend some time with the wise man and members of the family?

Upon meeting Swami Ji, I took an instant liking to him. His endorsement of my work led to my being swamped with business on unexplainable phenomena in the Fort Collins area. Moreover, I never lacked for exceptional home-cooked feasts from the Indian community of Fort Collins. Little did I know that my introduction into their customs and beliefs would lead me eventually to the most outrageous story of my life.

KNOWING THE UNKNOWN

A library of books exists that discusses haunted places around the world. Entertaining as such stories may be, there's a component of this phenomenon that rarely, if ever, gets addressed: Why do such phenomena show up in the first place?

If the swami had not been visiting Nisha's house, her ignorance of being haunted would have left her as contented as a baby in a crib. Until you become aware that the bars are a dolled-up prison, toys are all you need to keep you ignorant of living in an imprisoned world.

Three components led to the haunting of Nisha's home: (1) a portal that allowed the ghost to enter into ordinary reality, (2) a ley line that energized the portal next to the fireplace, turning it into a glorified radio station, and (3) a human (or humans) whose vibrational patterns of pity resonated with and attracted the spirit whose life had been patterned on dysfunctional pity.

Portals no longer reside solely in the dominion of the metaphysical. Over the last decade, discoveries in quantum physics made mathematicians and physicists alike realize we live in multiple dimensions. Though opinions differ as to just how many dimensions, the most common opinion is that we reside in eleven or twelve dimensions, not three. In string theory, one of the dominant models in explaining the barriers that make up dimensional boundaries is what are called p-branes (or dimensional membranes). The letter "p" indicates how many dimensions are involved.

At the heart of string theory resides the fundamental notion that teeny-tiny little strings are vibrating. Depending on what number "p" is, the vibrating string can be open (filaments) or closed (circular or geometric). These strings make up all of matter. What gets rather interesting is that theoretically these infinitesimally small strings can explode in size, creating a large hole (enclosed) within the p-brane. Think of it as someone slowly poking their finger into a soap bubble, thus creating an entryway into the inside of the bubble. The hole in the bubble is similar to a hole in a p-brane. Portals are like this. Instead of a soap bubble membrane, these holes are openings between dimensional worlds or dimensional realities. And what makes up these worlds or realities is consciousness itself. Thus portals are indicators of two worlds of consciousness opening into one another.

Different kinds of "fingers" can create these dimensional holes. Mother Nature can choose to create an opening between worlds (usually because she needs balancing energies or balancing frequencies, which can sometimes only be acquired from another dimension). Humans, with the power of intent, may do the same. Sometimes, violent consciousness can punch an unwanted hole in a dimensional wall—what I call a "rip." In my experience, any portal created with negative intent needs to be closed. And the sooner the better.

Remember how the dowsing rods indicated that I should not close the portal in Nisha's basement? That's because this portal had been created by natural means and was serving a natural purpose. The red rock fireplace contained high amounts of iron and crystal. Whenever the ley line intersected the fireplace, it excited the rock into creating a vibrational phenomenon, which turned into a portal that then broadcast whatever vibration came through it. A ley line, like any clime in nature, gently moves and sways along its path, not venturing far from its main byway. When-ever the ley line and the fireplace interacted, the portal opened.

The fireplace had literally turned into a radio station, attracting any consciousness that wanted to listen or, in this case, feed. Because of the karma and the resonant vibrations of dysfunctional pity in the house, whenever the portal opened, the ghost had access to the very vibrations it had lived with and lived on when it was alive. This vampire "feeding" allowed the ghost to sustain a consciousness that kept it locked in its own self-made prison. The irony of this entire story is that I had been called in solely to get rid of a ghost; in actuality, I ended up bringing awareness to those in the family who were making the very same mistake the ghost had made.

By placing intent into the rose quartz, the crystal held the vibration of the intent. Placing crystals on both sides of the fireplace shifted the vibration around the portal to a higher frequency, making it impossible for any aspect of consciousness with low vibrations to pass through. Think of it as taking a radio that can receive dozens of radio stations, and transforming it into a radio that can receive only one station, KLUV. The intention I placed in the rose quartz allowed only vibrations of consciousness that were centered in love.

There is true beauty in life. What looks frightening at first blush often turns out to be a blessing in disguise. We have only to recognize that. Eventually, Nisha hired me to return and work with her family. What ensued was the terminating of the karma that had put the entire family into self-made prisons of pity and fear. Their addressing their fear of the unknown within themselves infused in them the possibility of finding healing through their own giftedness, their own innate power, their own self-discovery that life is to be embraced, not feared, not chained to pity.

What I didn't realize at the time was the clever role that the swami played in fomenting change by asking Nisha to bring into her presence a stranger capable of shifting the karmic vibrations in which she and her family had imprisoned themselves. This case also changed my life. For I began a journey cloaked in the garment of a real estate consultant only to find out that such a guise allowed me to enter the worlds of people who never would have invited me, who never would have seen the worlds beyond belief.

Chapter 3

THE FLYPAPER SYNDROME

To her dying day, my mother refused to speak of my death. She refused to understand the implications of my having been pronounced dead at eleven years of age. My own desire to try to comprehend the fullness of that incident meant nothing to her. She and my aunt had found me drowned at the bottom of the Ohanapecosh River during a large family reunion. Having waded into the water by myself, I had ventured too far out and stepped off a drop-off. No one had noticed. To this day I can remember every single second and every drop of water as I slipped into darkness. Never do I remember being afraid during my passing to the God Light. This unfathomable presence of love simply told me I had to go back. There was more I was to do.

What I didn't know was that I had been pronounced dead by the park ranger who had called for an ambulance. I lay on the ground covered by an army blanket, all my relatives weeping over the tragedy. As a little dog pulled back the blanket from my head, shrieking erupted as I started coughing. Ever since then death has fascinated me, perhaps even befriended me.

Elizabeth Kubler-Ross, a pioneer on the topic of death and dying, states that we are a death-denying society. Doctors employ all manner of technology to keep us alive, even if that means we go through continued pain and suffering to the end. The Terri Schiavo case revealed the national mania around "pulling the plug" in a highly politicized media frenzy about one woman's journey toward death. Families go through variations on this theme regarding the incredible drama that is unleashed when a loved one is at death's door.

Ironically, Kubler-Ross discovered in her research that most people die between the hours of 1:00 am and 4:30 am, not because death stalks through the night for victims but quite the other way around. She discovered in her interviews with patients who returned from death, that they felt a burden knowing that their loved ones did not wish for them to depart. Lines of people had entered their rooms, praying for them to live, encouraging them to fight, insisting that they could make it through another day. In truth, many patients know it is their time to depart but feel held back from their exit because everyone around them fails to understand that staying simply is not in their best interest. So the dying wait when nobody is around. And, it turns out, that the hours of death are the hours when their rooms are finally empty or the prayer chains take a rest.

In my return from death, I sharply remember not wanting to return to the world of the living. Never had I known the love I had felt with the God Light. Why would I want to leave that? And what was my first encounter upon returning to life? Weeping. Sorrow. Shock. From a personal point of view, I can vouch for Dr. Kubler-Ross's findings. When we are at death's door, oftentimes our loved ones go to any length to attach our souls to the flypaper of their longing to have us live beyond our time. Such was the case surrounding a new client.

THE STORY BEHIND AUDIOMAX

Unexplainable events kept popping up at Audiomax (a pseudonym) after their move into new facilities. An industrial-press company had owned the building previously. The purchase of the larger space and the clean brick structure was thought to be a smart financial decision. Except for one thing. They were losing customers, and didn't know why.

The economy could account for some of the decrease in sales but not the magnitude showing up on their books. To make matters worse, the plumbing in the men's bathroom kept flooding not only the restroom but also the main showroom next to it. Five different contractors had been brought in, and not a one of them could find anything wrong with the plumbing.

In partnership with the bizarre flooding was the repeated burn out of flood lights, some of them even exploding. These were not ordinary flood lights. After all, this was the main showroom, and those lights came at a very high price for a business that depended on sparkling visuals to match their excellent reputation for high-tech pizzazz. Three electricians had been brought in, and, like the plumbers, they could find nothing wrong. Audiomax was a high-end home entertainment company providing exclusive customers with private theaters and luxury sound systems for their homes or businesses. The owner, a visionary, had taken the company from what began as a hobby, to the A-list of home-theater entertainment, creating an international reputation along the way.

The real estate agent who sold the building to Audiomax also had a reputation to uphold. Audiomax let him know that the building had become problematic, and they were not happy. That's when the realtor gave me a call. At first, I resisted. What did I know about plumbing and electricity? But once I heard about the repeated flooding in the men's bathroom, my curiosity got the better of me.

Mr. Mark Kane (not his real name) greeted me with a grin on his face. His first comment explained the grin: "So, you're Denver's Mr. Ghostbuster." In spite of my trying to explain to him that I had nothing remotely to do with ghostbusting, he preferred to think of me as having come from one of his favorite movies he watched in the fabulous home theater just off the main showroom. Apparently, the sound effects in *Ghostbusters* made it a natural to show to customers. Plus, it was funny.

The theater's opulence reminded me of once having sat in a new Ferrari. An old friend of mine convinced me he could talk a salesman into taking us for a drive. I had just been hired as a research and development engineer at Hewlett-Packard. Nothing seemed impossible at that time. So I accepted his dare, which would mean I'd have to pay for dinner and drinks at his favorite restaurant. Which I did—gladly.

After trying to shed the Ghostbuster comment from Mark, I further informed him that ghosts were a rare phenomenon, and nothing I had heard led me to believe the building was haunted. Nonetheless, Mark had taken precautions by having me come in on a Sunday when the building was closed. He didn't want any rumors spreading, and he didn't want his staff to know he had hired "Mr. Ghostbuster." When I explained to him that I would be using dowsing rods, his Cheshire Cat grin reappeared. Naturally, he preferred to use the more dramatic term for what I did: "water witching."

"Will those things tell you why we have repeated episodes of water flooding this part of the building?"

"They're just tools," I explained. "They help me work faster so I don't have to charge you as much." Honestly, at this point in my real estate consulting, I didn't come cheap, which he seemed to enjoy all the more. After explaining to him how I found the source of problems in houses and businesses, I let him know that I'd like to begin by checking the grounds outside.

"We don't have any problems outside. They're all in here," he insisted.

"I understand. But in my business it's not uncommon to find it's what's outside the building that's causing the problems inside the building. Not unlike the human body. Think of it as an environmental issue. Bad earphones or bad speakers can end up being the cause of bad hearing." That he related to.

As I prepared to dowse the large parking lot, I looked around at the other businesses surrounding Audiomax, checking for any telltale signs of any anomalies. Sometimes the most obvious indicators escape people's notice. On many an occasion I find cracks in the foundations of houses or large buildings that people seem to overlook. I follow the cracks. They tell a story. Denver is well known for its fluvial deposits. Clay soil dominates certain parts of Denver, and it is these deposits that cause the most trouble when torrential downpours create liquefaction where drainage is not taken into account. Not too many people know that Denver also sits on severe fault lines capable of creating superquakes every 300 years. The last superquake in Denver occurred over 300 years ago. So I take everything into account when I examine a piece of property.

What caught my attention right away were the trees along one section of the boulevard paralleling Audiomax. When a section of trees bends one direction while all the rest of the trees bend another, that tells me to check for ley lines. Trees tend to bend toward a ley line traveling through their midst. In this case the indicator hinted at checking the southeast corner of the building. Right away my dowsing rods picked up the magnetic clime of energy. Sure enough, the ley line went right through the southwest corner of the building and right through the main show room in the middle. Like an amateur Sherlock Holmes I continued to scout for clues.

This particular ley line tested out to be negative. In my work, negative ley lines can cause problems. As a metaphor, I consider negative ley lines to be magnetic in nature and positive ley lies to be electric in nature. In physics, one of the major forces is called the electromagnetic force. This force can polarize into two components, electrical and magnetic. Yet, they are both part of the same force.

I also check out the width of a ley line. Most ley lines in Colorado that I encounter turn out to be weak, only a foot or two in width. Major ley lines can extend up to fifteen feet in width. These I pay close attention to. The ley line going through Audiomax widened to about eight feet. To accentuate the situation, I noticed the power lines going into the building. Because the earlier occupant had been a press company, industrial-size power lines fed into the back of the building, not far from where the ley line exited the building. Putting this all together, I began to see why a dimensional anomaly might show up in the building. But there was one thing missing: no portal, no vortex, and no crystalline structure that might allow beings of consciousness to show up. Nonetheless, something had to be done about the negative ley line. I continued my search.

Just before entering the front door, a glint caught my eye next to the southeast corner where the ley line entered the building. At first I thought someone had potted a flowering bush on a trellis amongst the sparse shrubbery. But closer examination indicated some kind of shrine had been erected. A foot-high filigreed metal cross stood solidly amidst the branches of the flowering plant. *How weird,* I thought. Not knowing what to make of it, I returned to the main showroom where Mark awaited, eyebrows raised in question.

"Still checking things out," I said. "But I can tell you that you have a major negative ley line going right through your building and passing right through your showroom. I don't know yet whether that's causing your lights to short out. I'd like to check out the bathroom now."

Mark showed me the door to the men's room. "This is the bathroom that keeps flooding." As I entered, my body immediately reacted to an intense uneasiness, not unlike a feeling of accidentally walking into a bar completely filled with bikers wearing chains, their heads covered with bandanas.

"Wow," I said. "This I need to figure out." Mark folded his arms across his chest as I began asking questions through the dowsing rods.

"Can I ask questions while you're doing this?" Mark wanted to know.

"Of course. I actually like briefing my clients while I'm working. Sometimes the most unexpected information can come from that."

"OK. What's a negative ley line?"

As I gave my typical spiel on how the Earth's magnetic field works, in my head I continued asking questions via the dowsing rods. I'm one of those people who can't chew gum and walk at the same time. However, when it comes to my brain, I can have four conversations going on simultaneously, kind of like cerebral parallel processing. I've discovered I only have to listen to about every third word a person says to follow their conversation. On some occasions this can get me into trouble if I've missed one of the key words in a sentence. For instance, the sentence "Sacred **icons** from Byzantium **have** sometimes come from **sects** around Ionic Greece—made **with** colored **hues** that depict the culture," can register in my brain as "I can have sex with you." Really, two different conversations.

My brain jolted onto one single focused train of thought when the dowsing rods swung in with a *Yes.*

Did I just ask what I thought I asked? Rapidly my brain was tuning out Mark, and my answer to his question slipped from my mind mid-sentence. I had to backtrack to the question just asked. An alarm bell had just gone off. No parallel processing allowed. My brain went back three sentences to replay what had just set off the alarm.

Is the energy coming from a spiritual consciousness? I had asked in my mind (along with listening to Mark).

Yes. The rods had swung inward. Good. Another clue.

Is this spirit angelic in nature?

No.

Is this spirit ancestral in nature? This was a term I used to see if the spirit of a relative was trying to help out a person or a situation. I also used this term to check if a spirit guide was involved. Sometimes, the spirit of a deceased grandparent or a close relative is allowed to return to ordinary reality to serve as a spirit helper or spirit guide. I'll expound on that in a later case.

No.

OK. Not an ancestor. Is this spiritual consciousness a ghost?

Yes.

That's what had set the alarm off.

"What's wrong?" asked Mark.

"Hang on, hang on. I just picked up on something." I didn't want to tell him yet what I'd stumbled across. A part of me was still disgruntled over the "ghostbusters" comment, and another part of me wanted to make sure I wasn't trying to get even with him. Ego can be dangerous in the work I do. More than ruining your reputation, it can bring harm to a situation or a client if you aren't completely open and honest to the fullness of truth. What that means is that you have to give up any expectation of what you'll find. As a mathematician, I know my mathematician colleagues are still arguing about what dimensions five through twelve actually mean. Some are still debating about what makes up the fourth dimension. I've gotten to the point where I don't care who defines what. My job is to work with the metaphors that will allow some kind of truth to enter a given situation where other dimensions (dare I say "other worlds"?) are involved. The reason why realtors continue working with me are twofold: (1) What I do works even if they don't understand what I do, and (2) it makes for absolutely great water-cooler gossip. In either case, I *must* keep my ego out of the way.

Just to make sure I wasn't fooling myself, I decided to ask the question that had set off the alarm in a different way. *Is this a discorporate being that's in the bathroom right now?* I asked the rods.

The rods swung in.

Can I? May I? Should I find out information about this discorporate being?

Yes.

Once I discovered that the consciousness in the bathroom was male in nature, and quite disturbed, I decided to let Mark know.

"Well, guess what? There's a ghost in here."

"You mean the place is haunted?"

"Yep."

Mark burst out laughing. "My place is haunted." He guffawed again. "You know, I don't believe in such things. But this is soooo cool."

Great. Mark was living in a movie and I was being projected onto one of his theater screens. "But this doesn't make sense to me," I said. "The building just isn't that old. And from what I'm getting the ghost isn't old either. This shouldn't be a haunting. Plus, this guy is really upset. What would he be upset about? It's not like old houses where the spirit has a sense of ownership of the grounds or the rooms. Why would this young guy be so upset about your business or your occupying this space? I'm beginning to suspect that he died a violent death. But that doesn't make sense either. I need more time to untangle this."

"There's probably something you should know," said Mark, looking like the cat who ate the canary.

"And that would be ...?" I said encouragingly.

"I need to show you something. Outside."

Before I knew it, I once again stood in the negative ley line before the filigree cross. Mark revealed the story behind the cross. "Before we moved in, the realtor told me there was a suicide here. A young guy, for reasons no one knew, decided to plow his motorcycle right into the building at high speed. Apparently there is some kind of Colorado law that requires realtors to inform buyers of suicides or shootings or something like that on a property. You can still see the crash mark in the brick.

"The parents were inconsolable after the crash, and built a memorial to their son."

"This isn't a memorial," I interrupted. "It's an altar. Look at the way they've placed objects around the bush and the cross."

"Yeah. I tore down the original cross, and they came back and built another one. I tore that one down and then they erected this metal one. I decided to leave it."

I took out my dowsing rods and started asking questions. The answers told me this symbol of the parent's anguish and longing was the cause of their son not crossing over. "This has to be taken down if you want to get rid of the ghost. Energetically, this is what's anchoring him. The parents don't want to let go of their boy, and they have to. They have to let go of him so he can move on."

"Well, I don't think it's going to do any good to tear it down again. They'll come back and build another one."

After thinking about it, I posed the question to the rods whether the altar could be nullified energetically. Was the negative ley line contributing to the power of the altar of sorrow? Could some kind of block be put in place to stop the ley line? Could another block be put in place to stop the intention of the parents of forever hanging on to their dead boy? The answers all came back yes.

"The first thing I have to do is block this negative ley line. Negative lines are used by Mother Nature to feed negative phenomena, usually negative vortexes. If this line is feeding a negative vortex, it's not on your property," I told Mark. "These lines can drain energy from most human beings. I'm surprised the people in this corner of the building aren't having health problems or relationship problems."

Mark cleared his throat. "Now that you mention it, my top salesman has the corner office, and he's been having marriage problems lately. It's gotten in the way of his work."

"That's the kind of thing I need to know about. OK. The question now is where do I block this negative ley line? At the corner of the building? Or the edge of your property where it first enters?"

"Why not stop it all together? From the direction you're pointing it goes through that other large building southwest of us."

"I can't interfere with other people's lives. I only have permission from you to work in your life. In your case, this ley line is causing problems. Some people actually do better with these negative lines. It grounds them, keeps them energetically cleaned out. That's why I can't go past your property line."

"So what's the difference of whether you block it here at the corner or back there on the edge of the parking lot?

"I'm assuming that your employees park their cars in that area. It most likely isn't benefiting them even though they spend little time there. Those in the building sitting in the path would be affected more significantly. It can be quite draining to some people. Like me. The sooner I get this taken care of the better off I'll be."

Mark decided that I should set up crystals at the edge of the parking lot and under the power lines going into the back of the building. That having been addressed, I returned to the shrine of the dead motorcyclist. This kid had to be set free from the energetic flypaper on which his spirit had been caught.

I asked Mark if it would be OK to put a block in place around the shrine, using some of my crystals around the cross.

"You'd better hide them well. Cuz they'll most likely get rid of anything around that cross." And that's what I did.

After testing the energetic block with the rods and finding no tie from the cross to the spirit in the men's room, we returned to the showroom. "What I'm going to do now is attempt to send the son on his way. I'm going into the bathroom. It'll take me about ten minutes."

"Can I go in with you?" asked Mark with a kidlike grin. "I've never seen a ghost." This is the part of my work that I enjoy the most. Few will admit to believing in what I do, but that won't stop them from following me into the unknown. Whether they will admit to the authenticity of my work or not, they end up being changed by it.

"You won't see this one, either. It isn't that kind of ghost. You might see lots of water or hear sounds, but that's about it."

"Excellent. Now that would be worth the price of admission!"

I almost laughed. As much as people deny the existence of ghosts, they sure love to be around the thrill of facing them, whether that's on a movie screen or in a Halloween haunted house. We entered the bathroom.

As soon as I crossed the threshold, a wave of nausea swept through me, causing me to cough loudly. The kid was pissed. And I didn't know at whom. All I knew was if I didn't retreat I was going to throw up on the floor. As I did an about-face I slammed into Mark, nearly knocking him over as I charged back out the door. When I finished coughing, he innocently asked, "Something wrong?"

"I'm not sure you should go in there," I choked. "I need to prepare myself to try this again."

As I cleared myself of the nausea, I immediately started sending blessings into the bathroom and to the boy. Calm finally returned. "I'm going back in. I think you should stay here."

"Are you kidding? There's no way I'm going to miss this." The look on his face told me that he thought my theatrics thoroughly beguiling.

"Suit yourself," I said as I once again crossed the threshold into the men's room. Even though the atmosphere felt suffocating, I could handle the oppressiveness of it.

"Is he in here?" asked Mark.

"Oh, yeah. And he's not happy."

"Are we going to see green puke or anything like that?"

"This isn't *The Exorcist*," I stated matter-of-factly. I decided to sit on the tiled floor and appraise the situation. I knew the dowsing rods wouldn't work with this much charge in the air. I had gone through that in past cases. I needed time to handle this using my clairsentience.

What I was able to discern was that this young man had died before his time. Far-reaching consequences can arise from a soul deciding to commit suicide. The act of terminating one's own life can mean that one has decided to go against the Divine Plan that the soul had agreed to in the first place. To willfully choose to terminate a life journey can mean that the soul has chosen to make that life meaningless, that journey worthless. The outcome of such a choice is often that the soul will have to return immediately to the physical realm to incarnate, and live the same kind of life all over again. When a spirit discovers this, the emotional impact can cause deep regret and shame to emerge. It means the soul has failed at its purpose, leaving behind devastating results for others who had tried to help that soul in its latest lifetime. This was the case with the son. The parents had tried everything they could to help their son. They loved him deeply. To make matters worse, they blamed themselves for his death.

"What is that smell?" asked Mark.

"I'm not smelling anything," I answered. "What's it smell like?"

"Sewer gas. It's getting stronger. I think the plumbing is about to overflow again. Maybe we should get out of here unless you don't mind sitting in sewage."

"We'll be fine. If both of us were smelling it, I'd be taking your advice. But since you're the only one, you can chalk it up to the disruptive energy of the ghost."

Mark began waving his hand back and forth in front of his nose while checking out an escape route. For once I wasn't the only one feeling the effects of the outlandish energy. I refocused on the emotional charge of the spirit. Without warning, screaming filled the air—a piercing cry of a man who felt he had no outlet for his anger, his frustration, or his torture other than to wail like a banshee. Immediately I covered my ears only to discover it did no good. The agonizing sound pounded through my head.

"What?" asked Mark.

"You can't hear that?"

"Hear what?"

"The screaming." I was now shouting to hear the sound of my own voice. Mark looked at me as if I had lost my mind.

"I don't hear anything ... but the sewer gas has gone." He continued watching me, half expecting another scene out of *The Exorcist*. I could tell.

When matters start to get out of control for me, I bring in my angels. It was time to ask for help for this poor kid. My heart was breaking from the grief he was feeling. As the screaming subsided, I discerned more information about his death. He had suffered from manic-depression or bipolar disorder. In a fit of deep depression he had determined that he could no longer live in a world of hopelessness. The motorcycle had been his only joy. And like two lovers in a death grip, he had chosen to take his lover with him as he smashed into the brick wall of what was now Audiomax.

As I watched all this in my mind's eye, I knew that neither he nor his parents had been responsible for the death. The mental disorder had been part of the lesson he came to live in this lifetime. If the parents had only realized that his life had been completed rather than tragically terminated, he would not still be held on the flypaper of needless guilt that prohibited him from moving on in his journey. The overflowing water had been symbolic of his spirit needing to be cleansed of the guilt he felt for his parent's grief, cleansed of the stain on his soul that kept him stuck to them.

The outpouring of love from the angel washed over him, showing him the truth of what I had seen. Slowly, reluctantly, he released his attachment to having wronged his parents, to having ruined and wasted his own life. What the angel was imparting to the son is what Elisabeth Kubler-Ross, M.D., states in her book, *Death: The Final Stage of Growth* (Scribner, 1997):

> Death is the key to the door of life.... It is through accepting the finiteness of our individual existences that we are enabled to find the strength and courage to reject those extrinsic roles and expectations and to devote each day of our lives—however long they may be—to growing as fully as we are able. We must learn to draw on our inner resources, to define ourselves in terms of the feedback we receive from our own internal valuing system rather than trying to fit ourselves into some illfitting stereotyped role.... You can be yourself only if you are no one else. You must give up "their" approval, whoever *they* are, and look to yourself for evaluation of success and failure, in terms of your *own* level of aspiration that is consistent with *your* values. Nothing is simpler and nothing is more difficult.

The son began to see the full message of the angel. A growing light surrounded him, and he faded away, finally moving across the bridge of light to continue his living journey. The energy in the bathroom shifted like the dying of the night as it yields to sunrise. The only sound in my ears was the breathing of Mark. "It's over," I told him. "He's gone."

"Just like that? What happened?" Mark was not going to see a reenactment of the final scene from *Ghostbusters*. Disappointment pulled at his face.

"The boy finally realized the reason for his death, and it had nothing to do with suicide."

"How'd that happen? The lights didn't even flicker."

"I brought in an angel that showed him the truth and purpose of his life. That made him realize that his attachments to guilt and shame were worthless, serving neither himself nor his parents. The angel escorted him across the divide."

Though Mark didn't believe a damn word I said the whole time I scrutinized Audiomax, what he did believe in during the coming weeks was the return of his sales to normal, the cessation of flooding in the men's room, and the end of costly spotlights exploding in his showroom. Not once did he complain about paying my fee. I would have liked to believe it was because of the work I did. But I knew better. What he loved was the entertainment factor. This was a man who made his living in the entertainment industry. And I had provided him one of the most entertaining weekends of his life.

KNOWING THE UNKNOWN

It's a rare human being who can talk about the riches of death. But I am one of them. Not only have I walked through death's door and returned, I have sat with those who did not return—the moment when death slowly approaches like a long-lost friend, no longer wearing midnight clothes torn into rags by those clawing for lingering life. No, it's the kind of death that draws near with an undeniable light, glowing with the unmistakable grace of unconditional love. Several times have I seen the awe-inspired smile on those about to cross the great divide that truthfully has no division.

In Kubler-Ross's research she reports that her patients' last words reveal visions of past relatives coming to the bedside to assist in the escorting over. Most often reported—and most often joked about—is the appearance of brilliant light emanating divine love in which the soul enters. In spite of the archetypal fear surrounding death, these reports indicate there is nothing to fear but our own reaction to the unknown.

My suggestion, to those who wish to enter into prayer for dying loved ones, is to precede the prayer with the following precursor: "If it is in this person's highest good and best interest, I pray that ..."

What was unusual about this case was the ways in which all the facts appeared adorned in rags, when in reality a tuxedo lay hidden underneath. Normally a negative ley line running through a home or a business is a tip-off that there is trouble afoot. However, the true purpose of negative ley lines in nature is to remove, to clear out, to take away. Like the water flooding the men's bathroom, the negative ley line was potentially serving a purpose for the young man on his motorcycle to remove the burdens and attachments that needlessly were dragging him down into an abyss worse than the medically-based depression. When his spirit could not let go of the burdens and the parents couldn't let go of their son, we have what I call the "flypaper syndrome." Everything gets stuck. The flypaper is made of attachments to beliefs that are not our own. It's what's behind Kubler-Ross's statement "You can be yourself only if you are no one else."

Have you ever heard the classical philosophical question: "What happens when an irresistible force (the motorcycle) meets an immovable object (the brick wall)?" The oft-given answer is that one of them has to move into the past. In this case, both the son and the parents (with their altar of memories) moved into the past and remained stuck there. The best way to become unstuck is to become aware. In the case of the son, this awareness came through an angel.

The irony of this story lies in the role that Mark played. His childlike curiosity served everyone involved, even though he didn't believe any premise on which his business troubles had been based. The mere fact that he didn't get in the way of what transpired was enough for other forces to move into play, especially the angels.

Because I work with angels so often, the questions I most often hear have to do with them. Even though I constantly talked to my guardian angel when I was a boy (my nickname for him was Odin), I never really could see them or hear them until much later in life. That's because of my being so scientifically oriented. The first lesson I learned in working with the angels is what I call the "get-it rule." It's simple: "Ask not, get not." Angels do not interfere in our lives. We are free-will beings on a free-will planet. If we wish help, we need to ask for it.

Guardian angels can guide and protect based on agreements we make before we are even born. In Michael Newton's book, *Destiny of Souls* (Llewellyn Publications, 2000), his research shows the great lengths we go to in setting up the scenarios in our coming lives that will teach us the most and bring our souls the most helpful lessons. Once those are set in place and we find ourselves born into the world, the angelic realm is free to assist us in our pre-decisions. Though I have to be honest here: Newton completely dismisses the very existence of angels because one never showed up in his research. My response to that has always been, "If you want to find an Eskimo, you don't go looking in Grand Central Station."

So why ask an angel anything if you don't know how to get the answer? The way I started was with what I call "body dowsing." It's clumsy and whimsical but it's an easy place to start. You simply place both your hands over your belly button (technically called the "lower dan-tien"), and pay attention to your balance. What I have classroom participants do is first find out the name of their angels. The first power that the Divine gave to humankind was the power of naming (Adam was given the power to name the animals). If you know the name of any spirit, you have charge over that spirit. The reason for that is that the name is the doorway to the spirit's purpose. If the spirit gives you its name, it means that it honors your free will and will subject itself to your free will. It will not violate the sacredness of who you are. So I always go for names whenever I'm working with any kind of consciousness outside the human body.

First ask what the beginning letter of the name is, then pay attention to your body. Typically, if you ask, "Show me a yes," the body will lean forward. When the body leans backward after asking a question, that means no. Some people will work opposite to that, but you get the idea. Rather than go across the entire alphabet letter-by-letter, use what is called a binomial tree. Keep dividing everything in half. "Is the first letter in the first half of the alphabet?" If you get a yes, then find out if it's in the first quarter or the second quarter of the alphabet. That gets you get down to six letters, which is much more manageable. Keep in mind that this is a rough way to begin to get information. If the letters don't make sense, then find names that use most of the letters and ask if that's the name. Oftentimes you can guess the name with only a few letters. And there's a reason for that. Angels aren't hung up on names.

I remember laughing over an example of that in one of the books I co-authored, *The Masters Return* (Angel Gate Publishing, 2006). Joe Crane had just seen his second angel, who looked different from the original angel in that the angel's visage looked Arabic, plus it was surrounded by a yellow light. Joe had a pretty good idea it might be Gabriel but asked if the angel would tell him its name. "You may call me whatever you like if it helps you to know me."

Instead of asking the angel if he was Gabriel, he said, "I will call you Bob."

"As you wish," was the reply.

Joe had hoped for a smile or a laugh. He was that kind of guy. "Unless I am mistaken, you are the one known as Gabriel. You are the one that gave the world Islam."

"I have served God as this one before," came the reply. This interlude strongly illustrates what I have seen repeatedly: The angels mostly care about how they can help us. Even though naming is important, it's how we choose to relate to them through that name that is key.

Once you have the angel's name, you can then get into asking questions of the angel. Here are some pitfalls to avoid. Never ask an angel how you should live your life. They simply won't answer. We are here to live our own lives, not be told by another. I find it always a good idea to ask ahead, "Can I, may I, should I get this information?" That's an easy way to stay out of trouble. It's too easy to think we are hearing from our angel when in fact we are having a great time playing with our ego—which is another good reason to ask the above set of questions.

Don't ask angels anything that has to do with time. If they tell you, "Soon," I've found out that soon to them is not the same as soon to us. Their soon can be years. Time doesn't exist where they come from. So save yourself heartache and stay away from time questions.

Don't ask angels for lottery numbers. My biased attitude is that "the lottery is a tax on the mathematically stupid." Don't ask angels to participate in the stupid. Do you realize how many people are praying that their numbers will win? Do you realize that such imploring by thousands and even millions is coming from people begging for you to lose? Don't ask an angel to choose between you and thousands of others whose interests are counter to yours.

Don't ask angels how to run a business. I have been driven to near madness by people who ask angels about marketing questions that end up being opposite to what I have recommended. Angels don't fathom money. And they don't fathom profit. So don't even go there. The answer you'll get from an angel on profit will have nothing to do with the kind of notion *you* have of profit. "What profit a man if he ..." (Matt.16:24-28).

I have no problem drawing a line between me and the angels. I have often said to them, "If you think it's so easy being human, then let's see you incarnate and come down here." That dare has never been dignified with an answer, as far as I can tell.

As rough a medium as body dowsing is, there are many other versions of dowsing that work better for some people. There is finger dowsing, pendulum dowsing (what some call "pendeling"), L-rods (what I use), V-rods, bobbers, willows, straws, etc. The library is full of books on dowsing. Since I do not consider myself a dowsing master, I'm not going to scribble any more pages on that topic. I recommend finding other sources, including other people far more adept than I on this subject. Even then, I want to emphasize that I strongly consider dowsing a means to an end in working with angels. Ultimately, after enough practice, almost anyone can start to see or hear, or even smell, their angels. Yes, smell. I have one client who can literally call her angel in and fill any room with the smell of orange blossoms. It's great table talk at a restaurant.

In a later section I'll give details on how one creates a space in one's own consciousness for communicating with their angels, spirit guides, or other-dimensional beings of consciousness using holodynamics. Once people realize that they have access to other levels of consciousness, whether that be with their angels or their own higher consciousness (what some call the "superconscious"), a whole new topic comes into play: To be aware is to know, and to know is to become responsible. In my years of working with clients, I have found that this single word—responsibility—is the single greatest block to people moving into their power.

That's what I liked most about Mark. Even though he chose not to take seriously the work I was doing, he took complete responsibility for bringing me into the unexplainable. Even after the unexplainable events ceased, Mark did not feel it necessary to change his belief systems. Which I am fine with. What mattered was his taking responsibility. And all benefited.

To this day I imagine Mark still showing off his luxurious home theater systems to high-end clients, still relying on the movie Ghostbusters to illustrate the sound quality. At the end, I hear him saying as an aside, "You know we had a ghost in here once."

Chapter 4

THE HOUSE THAT SOLD ITSELF

The most bizarre cases I have encountered have involved children or teens. Roughly one-third of my cases come about because children notice strange anomalies within the home and eventually say something to their parents or exhibit such stressful behavior that a parent eventually sits down with the child to find the cause. The days are over when such episodes could be dismissed with "Oh, you must have had a bad dream." Or "You must have imagined it." What I call the "Quantum Generation" is here to bring change, and they will not be denied the new world they seek.

Author and columnist Sharon Begley states in a *Newsweek* article "The IQ Puzzle" (May 6, 1996), that "IQ scores throughout the developed world have soared dramatically since the tests were introduced in the early years of this century.... The rise is so sharp that it implies that the average school child today is as bright as the near-geniuses of yesteryear."

Bestselling author and colleague, PMH Atwater, LHD, PhD, takes this finding even further in an article written for *New Dawn* magazine (March-April, 2004) entitled "Children of the New Millennium." She points out, "Surprisingly, the gene pool cannot change fast enough to account for this leap, so we can't claim genetics as causal. Test scores rose only slightly in the area of rote schooling, so education isn't the cause either."

Atwater focuses on the fact that educators are puzzled as to why IQ tests have rocketed. But what I find most telling is in her observation: "The scurry to find answers to what is happening to our youth centres around one glaring fact: the extreme jump in intelligence, between 24 to 26 points, concerns 'nonverbal intelligence'—the ability to know or intuit information."

From my own heuristic perspective, I find Dr. Atwater's finding dead on. The Quantum Generation cannot be explained and cannot be defined. Their abilities are a phenomenon beyond typical explanation because they themselves walk in a world beyond the five senses. Atwater goes on to say, "This means the new children are natural 'creative problem solvers.' Yet in the area of genius, once ranked with scores between 134 to 136 points (some say 140), a preponderance of today's youth regularly test out at 150 to 160; many over 184. No precedent exists to explain this."

Indeed, I find myself in good company with PMH Atwater. These children I have been called in to deal with are without precedent.

In one of my cases, a real estate agent in Northern Colorado had contacted me after hearing about my work with other realtors. A client who had recently bought a house from him swore up and down that the house was haunted. Rather than dismiss the allegations by his past client, the realtor sought to keep his client happy, and, after asking around, decided to make an appointment with me over the phone. At the time, I was working on another book and felt compelled to limit my number of real estate appointments to twice a week. So my initial reaction was to either pass him on to a colleague or solve the problem over the phone. By this time in my journey with the nonordinary, I knew I could use my dowsing rods no matter how far away a client might be or how long the time had been since an incident.

While tacitly querying my rods, I decided to ask the agent, "Is there a teenager in the house?"

"Yes, there is. A teenage son of the father. The woman of the house is his girlfriend," came the answer. "She's the one who contacted me."

"The house isn't haunted," I stated abruptly. "It's an anomaly I call a 'false-haunting.' The boy is quite upset with his father and is using his abilities to create what looks like a haunting. I've seen this before, especially around children who have recently entered puberty." I thought that would be the end of the consultation.

A pregnant silence drifted over the phone. "Uhh, how'd you know?"

"It's what I do," I said, wanting to keep the conversation short. I had a book to get back to, and felt the sooner I gave the broker the info he needed, the better. End of conversation. Send me a check.

"The kid has turned into a Goth," the agent continued. "He and his dad are at war with one another."

"Well, Dad has to get over it. What I'm getting is that the son is tremendously gifted, and the dad can't see it." Once again I waited for him to ring off.

"Would you be OK with talking to the girlfriend? She was the one who told me about the strange goings-on in the house. I think she would be interested in talking to you about this."

THE STORY BEHIND CLIENTS LAURA AND MAX

After agreeing to speak to the girlfriend, whom I will call Laura, I had to take a closer look as to why this case could not be handled with a mere phone call. Over the years, I have learned to pay attention to my clients from the perspective that oftentimes it is the student who teaches the master. Why was I being drawn into this case in spite of my efforts to avoid it?

When I wrote *Indigo Rising*, it was an attempt to cast a different light on what was then called the "Indigo Movement" or the "Indigo Youth Movement." None other than my colleague, PMH Atwater, produced credible evidence with regard to the real gifts these children carry. She, too, disavowed the hype associated with this movement. As I began working with the Quantum Generation, I did recognize that wonderful abilities did show up in these wonderful kids, but not the way adults were portraying it. Indeed, I discovered the last thing these kids wanted was to be labeled. Their consciousness was not about impressing society. Quite the opposite. They came here to change society. What PMH writes about and what I displayed in front of audiences, was that the focus should not have been placed on the children but on their parents. My own frustrations in working with gifted children did not come from the children (who often told their parents that the parents were not in charge of them but here to guide them) but from their parents who wished to keep the status quo. The scandal from the overprescribing, overselling, and overmarketing of Ritalin caused those of us trying to empower these kids only to shake our heads in complete disbelief. Between 1988 and 1999 use of Ritalin in children had increased over 800 percent.[2] By 1996, the Drug Enforcement Agency showed between thirty and fifty percent of teens who were in drug treatment centers in Wisconsin, South Carolina, and Indiana, reported "non-medical" use of Ritalin. And where were the parents in all of this? Eventually, I had to stop working with youth because the real work needed to be done with parents, and the only way that would happen was if they asked for help. Which they didn't.

When Laura and I talked on the phone, she showed particular interest in my insinuation that the source of the "false haunting" was her boyfriend's son, Jason. After I told her that some teens can express impressive abilities as they enter puberty if they are emotionally distraught, she informed me that the son had been rejected by his mother after the divorce. The mother's own problems had consumed her. She was in no shape to even attempt raising a teenager. As we continued the conversation, Laura asked terrific questions that showed her concern and keen awareness of the boy. She had no trouble with his wearing Goth clothing and makeup, but her boyfriend took his son's displays as a rejection of the father and his values.

"This reminds me of a really bizarre case I was called in for years ago," I said to her. "At the time, a famous psychologist known as the 'Shrink of the Stars' asked if I would fly down to Los Angeles and meet with one of her clients, a famous rock musician. He owned a mansion in Beverly Hills that had served as a speakeasy during Prohibition. The entire downstairs had become quite popular to the Hollywood crowd in those days. Great music along with great booze made it a legend. However, for some reason, during certain nights, music from the

---

[2] *Frontline*, "Medicating Kids" (April, 2001).

Roaring Twenties could be heard in the upstairs master bedroom. And what particularly freaked out the wife was the appearance of flappers walking through the bedroom in full costume. She wanted to abandon the house. But the husband had sunk a considerable amount of his fortune into the property and wanted a ghostbuster to come in."

What I discovered upon walking the grounds was that I could see no evidence of a ghost anywhere. Since the wife had already left to stay with relatives, I decided to have a serious conversation with the husband. What I discovered was that they had a teenage son who had his own section of the mansion. When I asked if the son had displayed any paranormal talents, the father looked at me as if I had fallen through the roof. With great discomfort, he related to me that the son had shown a particular interest in strange artwork having to do with ancient times. When I asked if I might see the artwork, he took me into his son's room. What struck me immediately was that this kid was a wiz with electronics. He had all the latest gadgets that attached to the TV, his computers, and his musical instruments.

"'I gather that your son is quite intelligent,' I said to the father.

The musician proudly announced that his son was a straight-A student. That was, until recently. His grades had fallen off for no reason. But what I later discovered was that the parents were not getting along. I found out from the family's psychotherapist that the son also knew they were thinking of divorce, which upset him extremely. However, the son had said nothing to his parents. His emotional repression is what tipped me off. And once I looked at the 'strange artwork' the father had talked about, I knew immediately that the son was drawing what are called 'sigils,' or sacred symbols or seals. Even though his sigils had nothing to do with black magic, they were nonetheless sigils from the Middle Ages used by enchanters in the creation of love potions and love spells. I decided not to tell the father what the son was up to, but it did tell me that the son was most likely behind the weirdness showing up in the house."

As I continued to describe to Laura how I had handled the Hollywood case, she interjected with excited comments showing she knew the parallel I was trying to draw with hers. My approach in the earlier case focused on the father. I let him know that I had found a vortex in the bedroom—which in and of itself was not unusual. Vortexes make up most of nature. Even though the vortex was positive, I let the famous musician know that the music he was hearing from the 1920s was indicative of what I called a "screenshot"—projections of consciousness that can show up on vortexes as if they were movie screens, or echoes in a canyon—echoes that travel across time. The combination of the vortex and his son's ability to project his great unhappiness made for a warp in time and space. But rather than blame the son for the unsettling projections in the bedroom, I blamed the vortex so as to avoid any judgment within the family.

Using my dowsing rods, I demonstrated clearly to Dad how the vortex had created a space-time warp. As I traversed the expanse of the huge master bedroom, the dowsing rods would swing in every time I crossed the area where the vortex swirled from the ground through the roof. Dad grinned whenever the rods indicated the space affected by the vortex.

Such phenomena have been reported at civil war battle scenes throughout the South. In those cases, soldiers can be seen marching through museums. In other cases, sounds of gunfire and explosions can be heard as these projections across time-space find a "screen" on which to show up. That screen can be a human-caused p-brane (dimensional membrane), a power point (sacred spot), or a vortex.

What I had decided to do was to put in place a set of crystals that would keep any negative energy (the son's emotional projections) from entering the space where the vortex resided—stop the negative energy, stop the music at midnight, and stop dancing flappers from freaking out the wife. I laid seven different type stones on the floor in a geometric pattern called an "Angelic Gateway" or a "Gate of Grace" (*The Masters Return*, Angel Gate Publishing, 2006, page 23). Using my dowsing rods once again, I showed there was no longer any negative influence allowed in the bedroom. If Dad was OK with leaving the crystals on the floor, all should be well.

He readily agreed to do anything to keep the house, including explaining to his wife why I had laid out in their master bedroom eight stones in a strange geometry. After letting him know that the wife should be made aware of the son's deep concerns for both Mom and Dad, I left the detailed information about the boy with the psychotherapist so that she could continue to do intense work with him. Overnight the unwanted music came to a halt. The only time the flappers returned was when the housekeeper removed the stones while the family was on vacation, thinking they were the work of the devil. After being informed it was either her job or the stones, she left them alone. The Shrink of the Stars proved up to her billing, for she took the son under her wing to let him know how gifted he really was, and how important it was for him to express his anxiety to Mom and Dad, rather than taking on their problems and frustrations by using sigils. He had much he could teach his parents ... if they would listen. And in this case, they did.

I informed Laura that phenomena like psychokinesis, telekinesis, apparitional projections, and mysterious sounds can show up around troubled teens, especially gifted teens. There seems to be some connection between their first chakra opening up and the ability to release tremendous amounts of energy from an emotional source. She informed me that her boyfriend's son could get quite emotional. With this news, I felt I should have a look at the house. We set a date.

Laura thought it best that her boyfriend not be present due to his frowning on matters that couldn't be labeled as normal. From what I could tell, his life was anything but normal. Once I had a chance to go through all the rooms, everything I suspected proved accurate. But after sitting down with Laura and explaining why the ghostly effects were showing up, and describing to her in detail how gifted the boy really was, she felt that my explanations needed to pierce the ears of her lover. Long ago I had learned not to be afraid of any authority figure, so I agreed to meet Mr. Lumberjack, whom I will call "Max," before putting the house in order. Due to the ongoing war between father and son, the boy would not be present, choosing to stay with relatives for the time being.

As I arrived for the second meeting, Max stood next to his Dodge Ram truck. The two of them together posed like a pair of mountain goats, Max carrying a paunch that made him look more like a redneck than a civil servant—a fact I later discovered. When he shook my hand in a formal welcome, it took several minutes for the blood to return to my fingers. As I looked into his empty eyes, I found myself contrasting him to the picture I had seen of his son—jet black hair that stood up like a rooster's comb, skinny as a coat rack hung with black clothes. Dad had little hair except for the stubble on the sides of his head. The two were a regular Harold and Maude.

As Max ushered me to the house, Laura stood inside the doorway with iced tea in hand. Bless her heart, she remembered. Her great smile warmed me, her excitement showing as brightly as her lipstick. Her love for Max had created this coming together of voodoo and vanilla, a mixture she intended on turning into a family pudding.

After we grew comfortable with one another, thanks to Laura, I decided the best approach was to tell Max the scientific principles of why a house can seem haunted when in truth it's not. "We are at an unbelievable time in science, as well as history," I began. "Discoveries have been made that boggle the mind, and events are unfolding that our mainstream media can't begin to make sense of. There was a relatively recent discovery in 1964 in quantum physics, called 'Bell's Theorem.' Scientific journals and magazines like *U.S. News & World Report* have labeled this theorem the greatest discovery in human history. Yet hardly anyone has heard of it. Simply stated, the theorem says that all of life is one. Some call it the 'God Proof.' It's one thing for me to sit here and tell you this, but another matter if I can show it to you."

After asking Max's permission, I asked him to elevate one of his arms and show his strength as I pushed down. This time, instead of tilting a glass, as described earlier, I tilted one of the wooden chairs next to the dining room table, thereby shifting the feng shui in the room. And as described earlier, Max's arm had no strength when I pushed down again. As I set the chair upright, I tested the arm once again to show him that his strength had returned. "All of life is one," I pronounced boldly. "Even with a chair." The look on Max's face changed from shock to a grin.

"Do that again," he said. And I did. His only retort was, "That's the damnedest thing I've ever seen. OK. What does this mean?"

"I'd like to take this a step further," I said encouragingly. "I'd like you to see what happens when we humans put one another down or when we even think critically of one another. I'm going to test your arm once again, if I may." Which I did. Strong. "Now, all I'm going to do is think a critical thought about myself. It doesn't even have to be true. The mere fact that I choose to diminish myself, or for that matter anyone else, has consequences." I then made up a thought that I was wrong for imposing myself into this man's world. "OK," I said. "Now I'm going to test your strength again, just like I did for the tilted chair." His arm showed weakness once again. He looked over at Laura as if expecting some kind of explanation. The I-told-you-so look on her face provided little sympathy.

"All right," I said, "I'm going to reset you and show you the antidote to this."

I tapped my fingers on his thymus region, just above the heart chakra, to reset his body. Immediately I checked his strength again, which proved to be at full. "This time, I'm going to repeat the exact same thing, only this time, while I'm creating the critical thought of myself, I'm going to ask you to send me a blessing. It can be like 'I bless your heart,' or ' I wish you peace' or 'I wish you well' or 'I send you love.' Any of those will work. OK?"

Max nodded with approval. This time when I issued the critical thought of myself, he did not go weak when I tested him. "You see, Max, whenever I choose to diminish myself, I diminish everything and everyone around me. If I choose to diminish anyone else, the same result shows up. Please note the power you have in how quantum realities show up. By sending me a blessing, you nullify my own consequences in choosing to diminish myself. And in sending forth a blessing to me, you not only affect me but everyone around me in a benevolent way. This effect is known as 'quantum entanglement.' We affect reality for anyone or anything that becomes entangled with our consciousness. Now, the reason I am telling you this is so that you will understand the full impact you have when you criticize your boy or when you think less of yourself for not being a good-enough dad. I'd like to show you another way to deal with this dynamic between the two of you."

Based on the conversation I had experienced with Laura, I went into great detail with regard to the information I had discovered about Max's son. I told Max that his son Jason was greatly gifted in spite of how he appeared in public. The boy had been blessed with the gift of mercy— no ordinary mercy, but the kind of mercy that can change lives. Max's face relaxed into amazement as I revealed to him detailed information I had gleaned about Jason from my last visit with the dowsing rods—information that I couldn't have known about.

He looked over at Laura. "Did you tell him about this?"

"I didn't tell him a thing, Honey. He told me everything about Jason last time he was here. I just sat and listened. Now you know why I wanted you to hear what he has to say."

I continued. "Because your son carries this great gift, he tends to want to help everyone around him." Max nodded. "But because he doesn't have a healthy self-identity, he diminishes himself, which in turn reflects on you and anyone around him. His mother abandoned him. And at a critical time. He carries deep wounds because of this. And those wounds cause him so much pain that he lashes out at anyone who tries to love him. It's obvious to me that you love your son. However, he cannot accept this love because deep down he doesn't believe he's worthy of it. He tells himself 'Who could love someone that even a mother could not love?' So Jason's behavior makes no sense to you. And because it makes no sense to you, you in turn lash out at him. This maelstrom of negative reinforcement is self-perpetuating. It has to be stopped. And the best way to stop it is for you to send blessings upon your son."

I took a breath to gauge Max's reaction. The look on his face was that of a man who'd just walked onto a nude beach: What do you say? Do you stay? Or do you turn around and find another beach down the road?

"What would I say to him?" Max looked exasperated. "He won't even talk to me anymore. He lives in another world."

His bewilderment reminded me of past situations in which I had been asked by fathers to initiate their sons into manhood by way of what are called "rites of passage." I go into detail with one of those stories in *Indigo Rising*. In modern society, parents are baffled as to how to let go of the little boy who is no longer a boy. A part of them is terrified of losing the boy they have long loved—and equally terrifying to them is the new man standing before them—filled with societal rage over the loss of knowing how he fits into the world.

Because of those past experiences, I knew what to tell Max. "When was the last time you took him out into nature?"

Max looked at me with warming eyes.

Modern society has lost the ability to depend on nature to heal and to clear out disharmony. In literature we often read how pioneer men left the cabin after a family spat to clear their heads and get in touch with what really mattered to them. Nature will do that. The modern version of this retreat is for a man to go to the bar and down enough drinks to drown his sorrow. It only numbs, it does not resolve like nature does.

"Sometimes the best thing to say is nothing. Let nature show the way. When the moment presents itself, tell him that you love him. But do it in a way that blesses him for who he is. Affirm the man that he is becoming. Tell him what I have told you about his gift. Watch what his reaction is when you tell him a perfect stranger has seen this, and that you agree with that stranger. The main reason he seeks out the company of his Goth friends is because misery likes company. That company is joining him in telling the world to 'Fuck off and die.' Their black clothes are a mirror they hold up to the world around them: 'See what darkness you have created around us?' those clothes are saying. The makeup they wear is a mask that reflects back to the world the harm and injury it does in trying to make everything black and white, right or wrong, good or bad. Blessings don't care about such duality. Blessings go beyond wrong or right."

Max sat motionless for a minute. Laura had the biggest grin on her face. She thought this was going better than she expected. In truth, when I first saw the Dodge Ram upon my arrival, the distinct possibility of being thrown bodily out the door entered my mind.

"He used to love to go fishing," Max interjected, my thoughts of dusting myself off fading away.

I said nothing.

"But what about the crazy stuff in our bedroom? I saw the bed sag when this thing sat on it! You could see the impression in the bed covers. And then at night being woken up by something touching my shoulder. Creeped me out completely. I could feel the fingers pressing into my skin. This keeps happening. Are you saying this is because of my son?"

"I'm trying to tell you how gifted he is, not how cursed. If he can escape his dungeon of negativity and self-loathing, his wild emotions will yield to love, a love he can accept and trust. If he finds harmony within himself, then harmony will flow from all he does. Human consciousness is capable of extraordinary possibilities. Quantum physics labs are proving this true. A wonderful book for you to take a look at was written by Lynne McTaggart, called *The Intention Experiment: Using Your Thoughts to Change Your Life and the World* (Free Press, 2008). It's an easy enough read that gives convincing proof that humans are indeed the authors of the impossible. I've given you a taste of that today. If you can handle my showing you how all of life is one with this chair, then you can handle the possibility that a very gifted kid can foster strange happenings under your roof. Your son wants to change the world around him. This is not the first case I've seen like this, nor will it be the last. What I will do is clear the bedroom of the consciousness that has created these strange events. The rest will be up to you. How about you show me Jason's bedroom first? I think I should start there."

"OK," croaked Max, not sure if any of what I had said was to be believed. "This way."

As I followed him down the stairs to the lower level of the house, I wanted to tell him more about the world of the unexplainable into which I introduced him. But I knew from past experience that throwing an intellectual notion at an emotional issue was like trying to change a tire when all you have is an inner tube.

How do you make anyone understand the power of emotions when scientists are only now beginning to understand the monumental effect this part of our psyche has on what we call reality? Astronaut Dr. Edgar Mitchell of Apollo 14 fame, in a paper he presented entitled "Nature's Mind: the Quantum Hologram," states the following:

A powerful and telling series of experiments conducted by Dean Radin [PhD] (1997) at the University of Nevada at Las Vegas following a decade long set of equally significant experiments by Brenda Dunne, R. Nelson and Robert Jahn at Princeton University (1988) provide insight as to the subtleties involved in this level of mind/brain functioning. Jahn, Nelson and Dunn provided overwhelming evidence that subjects could intentionally produce statistically skewed results in mechanical processes normally thought to be driven by random processes. Radin went further; he discovered that audiences watching a stage performance would skew the output of nearby random number generators during periods of high emotional content in the stage performance.

Most people would look at such a statement and ask, "Well, so?" What people don't understand is that it is scientifically impossible to change a random number generator from outside its system. That's why computers use them to run everything from our national electric grid to the Internet. Changing a random number generator would be like trying to control a toss of a thousand pennies in the air, saying, "I only want one single penny to be heads and the rest tails." And then doing the same thing for the next hour. It just doesn't happen. What Dr. Dean Radin demonstrated was scientific proof that humans in high emotional states are somehow able to alter reality.

Work done by Stuart Hameroff, MD, and renowned physicist Roger Penrose, PhD, points out that humans are able to determine reality through consciousness, and that this consciousness is determined by the massive network of microtubules in our bodies. These microtubules, which coat our cell walls, are constantly changing. And the patterns they form by the trillions determine how our consciousness produces patterns upon the hologram of life, or what we call "reality." One of the most effective ways of altering these patterns is through high emotional states. In the case of swamis who levitate—counter to the laws of physics—their high emotional state is that of bliss. In the case of a gifted teenager in the throes of puberty, it's wild furor.

The research of Hameroff and Penrose implies that if enough cohesive consciousness holds an intent, that intent collapses what's called a "wave potential." In other words, if enough consciousness surrounds an intent, that intent becomes reality. Perhaps an easier way of looking at this is to consider the power of mascots at high-school games. In my case, the Purple Kangaroo served as our mascot at Lake Washington High School in Kirkland, Washington. When I first spied one of my classmates dressed up as a purple kangaroo at a basketball game, I thought, *Who on God's green earth thought that one up?* Honestly, how many of you have ever seen a purple kangaroo? What's so special about a purple kangaroo as opposed to green one or a magenta one? But there it was, a fully-costumed purple kangaroo running around the basketball court exhorting my fellow students to cheer for the team. After several games, I began to see the Purple Kangaroo as more than a symbol of our school's spirit and sports acumen. It became "real"—the symbol of the team became the team: "Go Kangs." After years of continual rallies with costumed purple kangaroos, Kang took on beingness, a personification of a collective-conscious agreement that walked among the halls of Lake Washington High. It was as if Kang were real. The mascot symbol had power, had influence, had purpose in defeating our sports foes. And it became so by means of the perpetuation of its myth, year after year. The myth became reality.

Such was the case with Max's son. The boy who was trying to become a man was able to create enough cohesive consciousness, using his emotional furor, that he literally created a being of consciousness. This being then took on the form of an invisible "thing"—a thing so real that it could even make an indentation as it sat on his dad's bed; so real it could cause the sensation of being grabbed by the arm in trying to get Dad's attention. This non-ghost that became a personified being of consciousness represented the son's desire to be loved unconditionally, to be paid attention to in a way that acknowledged his gift, his power, his place in the world.

Beds are symbols of destiny: "You've made your bed, now lie in it." Whether in dreams or visions or alternate realities, beds are a tip-off that destiny is afoot. Likewise, the ghostly fingers on Max's arm indicated to me the symbolic asking for embrace. The son was trying to reach his father in a subconscious manner that could not be acknowledged consciously by either the father or the son. They both wanted to be an important part of each other's lives, but could not crash through the barriers of self-judgment and self-deprecation by which each had become self-imprisoned.

When I entered the son's room, I immediately felt slammed by an oppressive negative force. It took me by surprise to such an extent that I immediately had to turn around and walk out to catch my breath.

"What?" asked Max obliviously, still standing in the boy's bedroom.

"The vibration in the bedroom is quite heavy and negative," I reported. "I need to do something about this. I notice your son's bedroom is directly beneath your master bedroom. If I'm correct, his bed is directly below your side of the bed upstairs."

"I guess that's correct. I hadn't thought about that."

"What I'm going to do is use sacred oils to remove this dark consciousness in your son's room. Then I'm going to close the door to keep the aroma in the room overnight. What I will also do is place a crystal in your bedroom directly above his bed. His bed is where I detect this low vibration. It should bring an end to all your unwanted events upstairs. However, we will still need to talk after I do this."

In the book *The Masters Return*, I describe how the angels give to one Joe Crane the formulas for making certain sacred oils and explain how these oils may be used in healing or changing circumstances for the better in our lives. Like the crystals that are used in making the Gate of Grace (or Angelic Gateway), oils have the ability to alter vibrations. This is no small matter when you consider that quantum string theory hypothesizes that all of existence is made up of vibrating strings. Everything that exists vibrates. If you can alter the collective vibration of an object, you alter how that object shows up in our world. Oils and crystals hold vibrations: crystals in a passive manner, oils in an active manner. This means you can place vibrations into crystals and they will hold them. In the case of oils, you can place sacred oils on a human body or in a liquid or on a solid, and by so doing change its vibration in an active way.

After clearing out the son's room and the master bedroom upstairs, I sat down with Laura and Max to review everything we had discussed. I reminded Max how important it was to send blessings to his gifted son rather than find fault or criticism. Equally important, it was mandatory that Max quit judging himself in a critical way as a father, lover, and as a man. This brought up two more topics.

Max informed me that his main concern about the house being haunted stemmed from the possibility that he might put the house up for sale. He'd purchased the house as a fixer-upper, and had put a lot of money into improving it. If the place were haunted, he believed he wouldn't be able to cash in on his investment. Anxiety increased for him because matters at work were not so good. His new boss had a personality conflict with him, thus causing Max to think about looking elsewhere for work. But with the economy so bad, jobs were hard to come by, and homes were hard to sell.

I took this occasion to remind him of the lesson that if we choose to diminish ourselves, we diminish everything around us. Rather than seeing himself in a difficult position with his new boss, I encouraged him to send blessing to his boss and the work environment he found himself in. If he could fully trust in himself, life would support him in the best way possible. In such an environment, nothing becomes a problem and everything becomes a potential for growing, learning, and acquiring wisdom. If he got fired, then he could trust that such a possibility would take him to a better job or show him a better pursuit of his purpose or teach him lessons in better becoming who he is meant to be. If he could eliminate the fear, then self-love and self-trust could blossom for him, as well as those in relationship with him, especially his son.

After I finished, Max looked like a quart jar that had been filled by a gallon bucket. Sometimes it's difficult for me to know when to stop, to know when someone can't take in any more information. I do the best I can and trust that the rest will take care of itself. With warm hugs, I wished both Laura and Max good journeys. As I drove away, I wondered how Max would handle all that I had flooded him with.

About three weeks later, I heard from the real estate agent once again. He wanted me to work with him on another property. In the middle of the conversation, he asked if I'd heard what had happened to Max. I hadn't.

"It's the craziest thing," he said. "He ended up taking his son out fishing, and the two of them had a connection like never before. The strangeness in the house has not returned. And to add to matters, Max was offered a new position in a different part of the county, which would require him to move. At the same time all of this was happening, I had a buyer who was asking for a specific type of house in a specific area. It fit the description of Max's house, so I suggested he take a look at the house even though it wasn't on the market. Within five days the house sold. I never had to post it. Max tells me his whole life has changed. That he's the happiest man alive. Him and his son have made great strides, and the son plans to move in with him and Laura." Added the agent, "You might get real busy given all the people he's told about you and what you did."

And sure enough, I got many phone calls because of the house that sold itself.

KNOWING THE UNKNOWN

When I first began working with gifted children, most were in their teens. Since then they've grown into adults occupying places of influence within our society. In their place, young children of today appear to be even more aware of worlds beyond ordinary reality. But what's increasingly confounding are the growing mysteries coming forth from quantum physics. We no longer are limited by the speed of light. In fact the speed of light can now be changed to be even slower than the speed of sound. When photons are slowed down below the sound barrier, they magically transform from photons into phonons (particles of sound). What this implies is that humans have, built within themselves, the ability to transmute reality. These gifted ones who have grown into adulthood seem to have built within them the innate sense of being able to transform and transmute.

In PMH Atwater's paper on "Children of the New Millennium and the Concept of Root Races," she writes the following about children who have been declared dead and have returned to life:

Additionally, of the child experiencers I interviewed from 1978 to the present time [2000], roughly 15% spoke of being here "for the changes." They were explicit in their descriptions of a time when the Earth and its people would need them—a time when they themselves would be parents or grandparents (depending on age when interviewed).... Finally I did some calculations, the difference between their age at interview and the descriptions they offered of that future time of great need. I was surprised to discover that a single timeframe was revealed—the years between 2013 and 2029—the first "light" of the Fifth Sun!

When Atwater talks about the Fifth Sun, she is referring to Central and South American Native prophecies that speak of a time when humanity will ascend into a world of greater consciousness and awareness, where the time of the Golden Age of Peace will reign.

What I am finding in my continued work with the Quantum Generation is that these Millennium Children who have grown into adulthood do see and do speak of the changes enveloping our planet at this time. They also speak of the changes we are all seeing and feeling at this time as our daily lives are turned upside down by new and higher vibrations surrounding the Earth. They also speak of a return to Eden and the shift that has already arrived that will once again open our eyes to our relationship with Mother Earth as stewards of this garden planet.

The story of Laura and Max have now become archetypal in their implications for our present world. It was no easy matter for Max to do an about-face in how he operated as a father and a lover. He not only listened, he heard. I wish I could say that all my clients operate this way, but I would be lying. As I continue this work, I find myself saying yes to requests fewer and fewer times because the time has come for my voice to be replaced by this new generation. If we do not listen to these new voices and if we do not hear them as well, then nothing will stop them in bringing forth change that will continue to turn our world upside down. If Max had not realized what kind of reality he was holding onto, he would have brought untold strife and pain upon his son. But worse yet, his son would have stopped at nothing in trying to bring change to his father, to change the one relationship that mattered most to him, even if it meant complete chaos. The false-ghost was merely a warning. If Max had continued to judge himself, to diminish himself—and because of that, diminish his son—he would have continued with a reality that would have ultimately destroyed his world. He would have lost not only his job, he would have lost his house, his beloved Laura, and his wonderful son as well. The Quantum Generation knows that all of us must make serious efforts at creating a world based on blessing instead of greed, abusive power, and exploitation.

I can't tell you how many of these new gifted ones are giving up, how high the suicide rate is among their peers. It's epidemic. These kids must be empowered or our planet will face the consequences. Data from ADASK (Alcoholism and Drug Addiction Statistics, Trends, and Costs) show that illegal drug use is on the decline. But ironically prescription drug use is on the rise, especially pain relievers. And kids are getting these prescription drugs by stealing them from their parents. Forty percent of teens who start drinking before age thirteen become alcoholics. You can guess where they're getting the booze. Teens whose parents talk to them on a regular basis about the dangers of drug use are forty-two percent less likely to use drugs.

What these statistics do not show is that the real problem is that the parents either cannot self-identify as to who they are and what their purpose is, or they have fallen to the national disease of self-judgment and self-criticism. Perhaps those reading this story will pass on to others the power of blessing and how it can literally alter reality. People must understand that there is hope, and *that* hope rests within themselves. We must stop diminishing ourselves based on belief systems that make us feel worthless or unappreciated. If we continue on our ways of self-destruction, the Quantum Generation will take that value system and turn it on society as a whole. And then where will we be? It's not too late to move into new awareness. Bless yourselves daily and watch what happens.

Chapter 5

LISTENING TO WATER

🖎 In Colorado there's a cowboy saying attributed to Mark Twain: "Whiskey's for drinkin', water's for fightin'." Even in the twenty-first century this adage holds true. English writer and historian Thomas Fuller put the concept of water in a different perspective that points at the politics and the value of this most precious liquid: "We never know the worth of water till the well is dry." Without water, there are no homes, there is no commerce, and there is no life. With too much water, there usually is destruction, or at least an unexpected cleansing. So whenever I'm called in to help sell a house or help decide whether a building should be purchased or invested in, water often plays an important role. The bottom line is that I've learned to listen to water. When I don't, it frequently means a storm is soon to brew.

The way I usually discover whether water is a problem or a blessing with a sale is through the five Chinese elements or *wu xing*: Water, Fire, Metal, Wood (Tree), and Earth. Though these elements can be seen as a branch of feng shui, they also can be seen as a branch of Chinese astrology (or astrology in general), another archetypal system I will use in my work. Archetypal systems can prove quite useful for bringing forth a language to address a troubling situation or to explain why a system is out of balance. Though I rail against belief systems, I don't hesitate to use mechanisms that will allow me to dialog with my clients—who often are devotedly attached to a belief system. Archetypal systems allow me a way of gently suggesting change to a client in a language they will not only listen to but also understand. For instance, I often am brought into houses realtors are trying to sell that were decorated by people who had psychological problems, depression being the most common. Rather than get into a dissertation on how the owners create belief systems originating from a medical condition, and how that medical condition determines the reality in which they exist, I get down to a description that covers all these concepts simply—the house reflects its owner. Never mind that I could put a realtor or a buyer to sleep jabbering on about the role of vibration from a string theory perspective, let alone getting into the science of vibrations from a quantum mechanics point of view. I simply tell the realtor that the living room feng shui is lacking Fire, which is code for "Let's brighten this place up, bring some energy in here." The feng shui needs to be balanced by bringing in color or adding more "energy" to the living room. The truth is that the living room is usually the first room a buyer heads to. And if the person who owned the house was dull in nature (medically-based or psychologically-based), they usually decorated their environment in dull motif.

My favorite real estate agent was Lily. She not only appreciated my input in her real estate sales, she also championed my abilities to look at real estate like no one else. Before I knew it, she had managed to bring to my stable six other top realtors, all from the award-winning, tops-in-the-business real estate company from which she operated, Pinto & Co. In the '70s, Mr. Pinto started the company, proving himself to be an honest yet shrewd land broker. He parlayed his success by bringing in other agents under his umbrella, allowing them to operate as if they were independent, while guiding them under his rules using his respected name and resources, all under one roof. Competition among the dozens of agents caused the agency to flourish. Because he held the power to decide which areas of Denver each agent operated in, doing well meant being assigned to the more wealthy sections of town, which meant even more income. The reward system he developed caused his company to acquire a healthy reputation among clients and competing real estate firms alike. Lily worked in one of the sections of town overseen by the top agent at Pinto & Co. As part of Pinto's mentoring program, Lily benefited greatly from learning from this top agent.

Because of her growing success, she began to invest in real estate herself on the side. She used me on cases where she wanted to determine if a property might be worthy of her spending her own hard-earned money. One of my most bizarre cases with her came from just such a query.

The house in question resided in one of the sections of town growing in affluence. Most of the houses had been built in the '60s using brick. With the growth of Denver's high-tech industry, more and more upwardly-mobile singles or young couples were looking for homes where their dollars would grow with the land values, instead of investing in condos or renting apartments. Renovation of such properties was proving quite profitable, and Lily was thinking of purchasing this particular home as an investment. Having recently been renovated, the home was still reasonably priced since the owner was looking to flip his investment quickly. But all that glitters is not gold.

When I entered the house, the first thing my dowsing rods picked up on was the low energy, which I choose to call imbalanced feng shui. Though the living room was nicely staged, all the colors snoozed in earth tones. "I can tell you that a male picked the paint colors for this section of the house," I told Lily. She smiled as she always did when I began pulling information out of thin air.

"Yes, that's true. He's done well with taking older homes and sprucing them up."

"Tell me what your feeling was when you walked in here the very first time." She began to describe how nice the place looked but that it struck her as a bit muted.

"Exactly," I enthused. "The whole house is done in earth tones, which in some cases is a good thing. But not with this house. The energy in this house is subdued when in truth it should vibrate. It needs vitality. So I'm going to suggest bringing paintings and floor carpets for certain areas with the wood floors." She accompanied me as I told her the best colors to use to bring balance to the various rooms of the house. What I wasn't aware of was the story behind the story, why the new owner had good style but muted expression.

As we stepped off the back deck of the house into the yard, my dowsing rods swung wildly. I froze in place as I determined what had set off the signal for me to pay attention. "Construction," I said. "There's a construction problem here. Something to do with these steps." I bent over to see if there might be rotten wood anywhere or some other defect.

Lily cocked her head as she stared at the deck, inspecting each section with a professional eye. "Oh my goodness," she bubbled. "I don't know why I didn't see this before, but this hand rail next to the stairs is out of code." She scribbled notes as I checked out the rest of the backyard. "This should be easy to fix," she chortled.

I should have taken the code violation as a hint. People who flip houses either are great at renovating because they genuinely love bringing a house back to life or they tend to be focused on making a quick profit and getting the house flipped fast—sometimes too fast.

The basement welcomed us as the last section for me to check out. The renovator had done a good job on the house. The areas of change I had noted would be easy for Lily to address. From past experience, I knew she loved it when inexpensive fixes proved to make a house more attractive and thus easier to sell. However, when I stepped into the laundry room area, the rods swung outward. I began asking the series of questions I normally use to find the cause: Electromagnetic? No. Geomagnetic? No. Spirit? No. Ancestor? No. Karma? No. Feng shui? No. Elements? Yes.

When I went through the list of five Chinese elements, water kept showing up. I began looking for leaks but couldn't find any; then for cracks where water might be oozing in from an underground spring. Nothing. By this time Lily knew I was searching for a problem.

"What's going on?" she asked in her wonderful can-I-help voice.

"Water. I keep getting water. And it's in this area. But I'm not seeing anything. There's a water stain here on the cement floor but I keep getting that this isn't the issue. This stain needs to be cleaned up or painted over, by the way. Do you know why it's here? Has there been any kind of water problem in the past?"

Lily pressed her pen into the dimple of her left cheek while she stared into nothingness. "Not that I can think of. However, the owner did replace the plumbing down here. Maybe there's something he missed? Is there a construction problem?" I loved the fact that she was using my terminology. She had paid attention when I discovered the issue with the railing. That's one thing I had already learned about Lily. If I advised that something be changed or fixed, she hopped to it. Oftentimes my recommending a fix seems to have no basis in fact, or seems crazy. Some agents tend to ignore those fixes. It's only later that the reason for the recommendation makes itself known.

"I asked but got a maybe on that. It's weird, because only one rod swung in. That means I need to ask the question differently to get a clearer answer. I keep trying to think of a different way of asking about the water but have run out of ideas."

"How about we look under the crawl space? There's a trap door over here. Let me go get an electric lantern. I always carry one in my car."

As Lily retrieved the lantern, I removed the covering over the crawl space. Shiny copper pipes glistened, announcing how new the renovation had been. Not a spider web was to be seen. Lily arrived with lantern in hand and began looking at the piping herself, even going to the trouble of crawling into the opening to spy areas in the far corner. "Everything looks pretty good. I don't even see any damp spots in the dirt that would indicate a leak somewhere."

Eventually, I had to give up. As hard as I tried, I could explain why the dowsing rods kept indicating water, water, and more water. Had I paid closer attention to the previous clues, I might have known what was about to happen.

Five days later I received a phone call from Lily. "Well, I now know why you kept getting water with that last house we looked at. This hard freeze we just had froze the pipes in the crawl space, and caused the basement to flood yesterday with the thaw." The temperatures had dipped below zero for three days, not unusual for Denver in January. The owner had to fix the broken pipes and install wiring to warm them when the temperature in the crawl space dropped below freezing. Before the end of the month, the house sold. Lily had decided not to invest in it. But her commission made up for that.

Lily's story about the water spread like a flash flood through Pinto & Co. For some reason, stories about my weirdness seemed to entertain the agents more than the usual gossip about the weirdness of new buyers, which in some cases were legend. Before I knew it, one of the agents had passed the story on to her husband, who happened to work at the Denver NBC television station. With a little research, he managed to dig up my email address and asked if I would be open to doing an interview on the local morning business report.

Normally, anyone would be thrilled to appear on TV. I didn't happen to be one of them. Because of my bestseller, *The Messengers*, I had learned early on how television works. Unlike newspapers, which I found to be loose with facts and long on finding dirt, TV was more interested in a good story. TV thrives on entertaining, while newspapers thrive on sensationalizing. My work with realtors and homeowners had become my sanctuary. I loved the way everyone benefited from my investigations. Sure, I was weird as a Swiss army knife but that was part of the fun, especially when the weirdness produced amazing results. I really wasn't in the mood for being TV entertainment, so I declined the TV producer's offer. Or so I thought.

THE STORY BEHIND JILL

Shortly after declining the TV interview, a wealthy client in the Santa Fe, New Mexico, area called me and asked if I'd come down to work with her. She specialized in real estate consulting as a hobby, usually on the interior design end, and displayed undeniable talent at how to make a house look spiffy. But she also had a great eye for a buy. One of her friends was thinking of purchasing a hacienda north of town, and she wanted to fly me down to evaluate the property. She informed me that the estate was a candidate for historical site status, with its legendary European gardens amid traditional Catalan stonework, including a year-round flowing stream. One of the early Spanish families had built the hacienda, having received a royal land grant from the king of Spain, which had been passed down ancestrally. The hacienda had fallen into disuse in modern times, and my client's friend was thinking of purchasing the property and restoring the grounds. Would I come down?

Santa Fe is like a giant playground to me. The arts reign supreme with tourists celebrating the grand display of talent during the day, and artists partying at night. Even though Santa Fe harbors a population of

70,000, it ranks second only to New York in art sales. Never have I witnessed a more varied culture than what dwells in the unvaried adobe motif of the city. It's amazing how many different building concepts and designs rub shoulders, all following the city mandate of adobe structure. It's as if the common sight of adobe buildings were intended as a backdrop for the explosion of exotic artistic galleries that light up the atmosphere of Santa Fe.

When Jill picked me up at the Santa Fe airport, she was already bubbling with excitement about a new antique she had discovered at quite a bargain. Jill's adobe mansion has more artwork than some museums. If she ever decided to live elsewhere, half the art community might have to go on unemployment. I loved listening to her. Compared to her, I was as exciting as adobe mud.

We headed straight to the hacienda. She provided me a history of the property as she whipped around side roads toward our destination north of the city. Driving with Jill was like attending one of her cocktail parties. The only thing that mattered was conversation. She drove fearlessly, paying no mind to the possibility that she could be ticketed in any number of a hundred places. Her Mercedes SUV drove like a tank on the county roads. I pitied anyone who might get in the way.

She informed me that the property we were seeing had been part of a very large land grant awarded by the king of Spain. The grant came through a military leader named De Vargas to a Spanish soldier named Zisneros who had helped in the recapture of lands from the Pueblos north of Santa Fe. With the treaty of Guadalupe-Hildago, which created New Mexico as part of the United States, all historical land grants were honored. The hacienda had been built by a descendant while major portions of land surrounding the property had been sold off. Part of the draw to the property was a large stream that flowed through year-around. Streams in Santa Fe County are jealously guarded, especially when one observes the once beautiful Santa Fe River running through town, now the size of a small drainage ditch. As I said earlier, no water, no city. Most of what was the Santa Fe River now flows through the faucets of the city's inhabitants.

As Jill drove into the complex of buildings, right away I felt embraced by its natural beauty. Even though many months of disuse had left the gardens dried up with tall weeds growing everywhere, the former grandeur of the lattices and statuary still shone through. Jill unlocked the door to the casa grande (big-house) to give me an idea of how much fixing was needed to restore the polish to the old place. As I wandered around, I began to feel an unease. When that happens, I normally get out my dowsing rods, but Jill was still in the middle of her tour speech, and when Jill speaks, you at least have to pretend to listen. The tension increasingly gnawed at me. When finally she took a breath, I informed her that there was something I had to check out. She had seen me work enough to know that as I exited, she had to follow.

A force pulled me toward the stream. As I stood on its banks, I couldn't help but notice the large boulders lining one side; probably to help during spring run-off, I posited. But as I walked further along the bank, the boulders gave way to concrete walls. It was there that the force seemed strongest. As I checked my dowsing rods, my greatest concern was realized. The force was a deva. And the deva was pissed.

The topic of devas is tricky at best. Many viewpoints exist regarding these beings, with some people treating them as demi-gods while others seeing them as fabled characters. Still others use the term interchangeably with angels.

I don't see myself as an expert in devas. I operate from my experience, as limited as it may be. My viewpoint runs parallel to the Purple Kangaroo I spoke of earlier: these beings are the creation of human consciousness. But that doesn't do justice to their role (or roles) as nature spirits or cosmic guardians. For I've discovered there exist many types of devas, ranging from house devas to animal devas to tree devas to land devas. This was a water deva.

In my terminology, I classify any creation evoked from human consciousness as an elemental. I first ran across this term in one of my "bibles," *The Magus of Strovolos: The Extraordinary World of a Spiritual Healer*, by Kyriacos C. Markides (Penguin, 1989). The magus that Markides writes about is one Spyros Sathi, also known as Daskalos, a legendary adept from the island of Cyprus. In the book on page 34, Daskalos describes elementals in the following way:

Elementals ... have a life of their own just like any other living form and can have an existence independent of the one who projected them. Any thought and any feeling that an individual projects is an elemental.... There are two kinds of elementals: those that are produced subconsciously ... called elementals of "desires-thoughts," and those consciously constructed and called elementals of "thoughts-desires."

Daskalos goes on to describe elementals of desires-thoughts as being a "characteristic of ordinary people who lack an understanding of the nature of thought and desire." Because of this, he asserts that those who create elementals can often fall prey to the elemental they created. "It is the law of Nature that once elementals are projected outwards they eventually return to the subconscious of the person who created them." Interestingly, Daskalos illustrates how such thought forms are the source of many habits and obsessions. He also states that the tendency of elementals to return to their source serves as the foundation for the Law of Karma.

Though others may disagree with my classifying devas as elementals, I do see them as guardians of the earth, created from humanity's collective subconscious as humanity chose to abandon its role as guardians and stewards of Mother Earth. This abandonment occurred not from willful abdication or human selfishness but from humanity's choice to focus on saving itself from its own descension into lower vibrations. Humanity's descending stemmed from the recognition that it had discovered the ability to transform darkness into light. The secret teachings of the Qabalah contain such a reference to humanity's discovery of transforming darkness. From that discovery we decided to ask the Lords of Arulu (the Lords of the Suns) to open further the gates that held back darkness so that we might bring forth yet more light. Our good intentions almost resulted in our own demise. But that is another story. The point is that as humanity fought for its own survival, it subconsciously left behind the devas to steward Mother Earth.

I'd like to make one more point from Daskalos's teachings. He taught that "the way an elemental appears depends on the language of the person and the place from which he comes." I submit that this may explain why the entire topic of devas can prove confusing or conflicting. Any devas I have seen appear tall with almost doughboy features made out of a mudlike substance. Others see them as brilliant beings of light.

As I stared at the stream flowing below me, I could not see the deva, only feel it. The disturbing vibrations it sent out struck me as being angry or upset. To someone else these vibrations might bring forth a different reaction. As I tried to discern what the deva was trying to communicate to me, Jill interrupted.

"Honeybunch, what's going on? You look worried." She spoke in her soft Kansas drawl. She could tell you to go straight to hell and make it sound like an invitation to dinner.

"Jill, what can you tell me about this stream?"

"Well, you know how important water is in these hereabouts. From what I've heard, the current landowner wanted to create a broader area of land on this part of the property, so he diverted the stream. That's why that cement wall is in place, to keep the stream from reclaiming this section of the land. When the stream floods, it creates quite a wash through here on its way down to the Rio Grande. Why? Do you think there's going to be a flood?"

"I'm not sure yet. There's a water deva here, and it's pretty upset. I think it's because of the stream being changed. Humans can be quite arrogant when it comes to nature. I'm not sure what the consequences are yet. Aren't there laws here about messing with streams?"

"Honeybunch, this is New Mexico. The laws governing water have a long history of corruption and greed. New Mexico's water rights are based on what's called the 'law of prior appropriation.' Roughly, that means first-in, first-owned. Because this land was owned before 1907, all rights revert to what the king of Spain gave the landowner. That means that the landowner here can do whatever the hell he wants with the water."

"The deva may have a different opinion," I mumbled. "Can we look around some more? Maybe I'll find out what this weird vibration is about by exploring more."

Jill continued to show me the rest of the estate, finding great delight in telling the history of the various artworks. As she took me into the guesthouse, I felt the energy grow decidedly negative. I began working my dowsing rods, which caused Jill to stall her role as tour guide. As I sifted through the information I was getting, I told her what I was picking up. "Jill, the deva has created another stream, an underground stream. And it runs right below this floor where we are standing. You see these water stains on the floor? The deva is going to flood this area eventually. In fact, I'm picking up that there is now mold in here."

That was Jill's signal to start pulling at carpet and loose boards. Sure enough, black mold everywhere. "Oh my gawwwd," she intoned. "This is not good. We're going to have to get someone in here to dry this place out with a blower. Clean this place up."

"I wouldn't waste the money," I said. "I believe you're only seeing the beginning of this. This deva won't be stopped. It will reclaim this entire piece of property one way or the other. The black mold alone will make this building uninhabitable. Let's go check the casa grande again."

As we checked the remaining building on the way to the casa grande, it became evident that black mold had already taken over from the underground stream percolating up into the foundation. With a second check of the casa grande using a bright light, Jill found black mold taking over most of the house. "Are you sure we can't clean this up?" she asked hopefully. "My friend is really taken with this property."

"Jill, I know you're good at what you do, but I think you'd better tell your investor friend to stay away from this property. It's my opinion that no one will ever live here again."

Jill would find out three weeks later that a thunderstorm would dump a deluge of rain. The stream would swell to unmanageable size, change its course, and sweep through the buildings of the hacienda, destroying all of them.

As we drove back to Santa Fe, Jill asked if I had enough energy to look at one more place, a new condominium complex. A good friend of hers was about to purchase one of the condos and wanted to know which one would work best for her. Much to my surprise, Jill informed me that the developer of the complex was the same guy who owned the hacienda. The complex had become controversial with several environmentalists objecting to the way permits had been issued. Immediately, my hackles went up.

In checking out the condos and the underground garage, I delivered a warning to Jill's friend. The condo I recommended she buy would do well, I told her; and she'd find great joy in the view of the nearby city plaza and the Santa Fe Trickle (River). However, I cautioned her that there would be water problems with some of the other condos on the south end. I also warned her that the underground garage would most likely have flooding problems in the southern section as well, but her parking space and exit would be just fine. I had already spotted cracks in certain parts of the garage foundation. She decided to buy the condo I recommended. And as I predicted, the same storm that flooded the hacienda also flooded the underground garage. Several of the condos ended up with structural damage from settling of the water-saturated ground around the foundations, as well as damage from black mold. The water deva had sent a strong message to the landowner—a message that would not go away.

Upon returning from Santa Fe, I found two messages on my voice mail from the Denver NBC station. The producer wouldn't take no for an answer. He stated that he'd talked to Lily while I was away, and that she'd be willing to appear with me. This guy was good. If I had a weak point, it would be Lily. I decided to call him, since Lily had obviously given him my unlisted number. In looking back, this was the time I should have trusted my instincts. The episodes in Santa Fe were more than meetings with clients: They were lessons in listening. There is a price to pay when people choose not to listen to nature. There is an even deeper price to pay when people do not listen to themselves.

The producer effused with enthusiasm about bringing together the realtor with the story behind the realtor. I made it very clear that the only way I would submit to the interview was if Lily were included. No Lily, no interview. Two days later I received a call from Lily. The producer had gone too far. Wanting to blow the story up even more, he had called Mr. Pinto, himself. When Pinto found out what six of his top agents were involved in, he hit the ceiling. He specifically aimed his ire at Lily. What was she thinking? he had screamed at her. What would happen to the company if word got out that Pinto & Co. was consulting with crackpots? He never bothered to check the sales figures for the six agents working with me. The only thing he could see was becoming the laughing stock of Denver realty. He forbade Lily or any of the other agents from appearing on camera or being quoted. Any agent caught working with me again would be dismissed. End of story.

In a matter of forty-eight hours, my vibrant real estate consulting business went from successful to non-existent. Lily was so ashamed, all she could do was email an ardent apology, coupled with a regret that she was too embarrassed to speak to me. Everyone suffered, including Mr. Pinto, as it turned out.

KNOWING THE UNKNOWN

In William Shakespeare's *Richard III*, he pens these words: "The people are like water and the ruler of the boat. Water can support a boat or overturn it." The real question in the Pinto & Co. story is "Who is the ruler?" Each of us has to determine what or who will rule our lives. Mr. Pinto's belief systems caused him to act only out of fear, rather than check the truth behind what was quietly happening within his company. To a man for whom sales meant everything, he certainly displayed blindness. However, he wasn't the only one. I, myself, displayed another kind of blindness in failing to trust my own decision about providing entertainment to a TV audience. Most entrepreneurs would die to get television coverage for their business. But the last thing I needed was more business. In fact, my schedule had reached the point where I was turning away business. When I decided not to listen to myself, I gave up being ruler of my own destiny. So why did I give in to doing the interview?

Throughout my life, I'd been the nerd, the weird guy. Growing out of that left me with a strong sense of rooting for the underdog, lifting up the little guy. I thought Lily would benefit from the TV interview. Repeatedly I have gotten myself in trouble for seeing the best in others when they weren't quite ready to see, let alone deal with, the best in themselves. People's lives are journeys. And those journeys must be respected. What I have had to learn the hard way is to let people arrive at their destiny in their own good way, and in their own good time. Just because I can see their destiny before they can, does not give me license to interfere and push them onto a fast track to the realization of their gifts or their full purpose.

Lily was a hero to me. Her skills as an out-of-the-box realtor brought her to the top of her profession. If she had stood up to Pinto, trusting in her own abilities to go it alone if need be, both he and she would have reached another level in growth. For as it happened, Pinto & Co. fell into palace intrigue. Because of the collapse of the Denver real estate market shortly after the debacle with Lily, Pinto fell back to his controlling ways. He ended up losing his top agent in the process, the one who had mentored Lily. Pinto's health began to fail, and rather than trust his top people to carry on his legacy, his obsession about control caused him to set up his son as heir apparent. Simply put, the son had the sales skills of a rottweiler and a nose for white powder. Pinto could not control his son, and in the process lost the true talent within his company because they refused to be controlled by a dysfunctional tyrant.

Lily became a fixture with the loss of her mentor. She feared rocking the boat. Yet if she had done just that at the critical time of the TV interview, her unusual talent would have placed her before the whole of Denver. However, my point is that this was not my call. The facts showed she was not ready when I thought she was. This is where the power of belief systems has to be respected in spite of my rejecting them. A second party cannot step in to take away a belief system of another. The holder of the belief system must be the one to release it.

Only now are people in the Santa Fe region fully listening to the waters. Groups have formed to restore the Santa Fe River. How will people get their drinking water? By being open to new concepts and new ways of working with the land. Quantum experiments in labs are showing that the observer controls the outcome of a reality. What the observer expects determines the results of the experiment. Across our planet potable drinking water is becoming less accessible and more valuable. Unless we break out of limited consciousness, our planet will end up facing what Santa Fe is already wrestling with.

The history of New Mexico water has led to abusive use of aquifers by corporations who still believe they can do whatever they want because they own it. Like the hacienda, this will change one way or another. Those capable of listening to Nature and hearing what she whispers are taking a leadership role. The mirage of belief systems are being seen for what they are—mirages.

Because of what happened at Pinto & Co. I walked away from any further work in real estate. Or so I thought. A flood of fear and judgment had washed through my land and left it wiped out. But water must be listened to, even when it floods. We must not let our fears behind our belief systems limit us, even in dire situations. When rivers flood, they do more than cause destruction of the old, they leave behind rich silt deposits that create a place of welcome for the new. In spite of recognizing that in Santa Fe, I failed to see it in Denver. Even I, am subject to being shackled by my own beliefs.

Chapter 6

THE PRINCESS AND THE FROG

In the original Grimm's fairy tale of the "Frog Prince," the princess changes the frog back into a prince by throwing the frog against a wall out of disgust. In the times of Grimm, this was one of the techniques in folklore for breaking shapeshifter magic. In modern times, Disney has chosen to have kissing as the transformational breaking of the spell. Whether one sides with the original tale where the spell is broken through disgust or the modern version where the spell is broken through affection, we once again find ourselves witnessing the archetypal altering of reality via emotional forces. But is that the only way to alter reality?

The Pinto incident left me disgusted. I missed all the fun and wonder in which I had once reveled, killed by the fears of one desperately holding on to the ways of the past. My consulting-practice prince had been turned into a frog. Further turmoil surrounded me as I decide to leave Denver and eventually accept an offer in the Fort Collins area where I now hid out. I have a repeated history of going into seclusion when I get fed up with the world. Why it repeats is subject to examination because escaping from life has never worked as an antidote to the pains of life. Yet here I was again repeating in similar fashion old patterns because of the grinch who had cursed my prince.

Like the shapeshifted frog in the pond, my self-imposed exile found itself disrupted by the arrival of a princess. Her name was Elizabeth. On the phone, her voice was that of innocence and sincerity. A close friend of hers, who was a client of mine, had given her my phone number. Over tea, Elizabeth had confessed to her friend a desire to face an old bogy of hers, one that she did not understand and had never been able to conquer despite her repeated efforts. She felt the need to bring in help but didn't know where to start. My past client suggested the phone call.

THE STORY OF ELIZABETH

When I parked in front of Elizabeth's house, out of habit I began absorbing information as if the house were for sale and I were working with a realtor. Caught by surprise, I froze in place pondering why. Did I miss my old consulting business that much? *Not really* was the answer that echoed in my head. As I stared at the Moorish arches that accented the Spanish architecture, I set the value of the home at around half-a-million dollars—another past habit. Oftentimes when I'm working with clients, the price of the home has a role to play in whether the house will sell. Sometimes the price needs to reflect the destiny number (numerology) of the house or its owner; at other times the price needs to be in harmony with the feng shui. As weird as my recommendations in price setting for a house can appear, it works. If nothing else, a weird looking number can attract attention to the listing. So part of my habit in looking at real estate was assessing what price should be set for a house. Oddly enough, when checking clients' previous listings, several of them had underpriced their homes. Raising the price resulted in the house selling.

Elizabeth's property stood out in the neighborhood with its clean look and wonderful energy. As I indicated before, homes tend to reflect their owners. Landscaping works the same way. One of the telltale signs of a problem inside the house is over-landscaping in the yard where one feels stepping onto the lawn might result in an arrest for trespassing. Elizabeth's yard emitted a wonderful welcoming sense to it—open enough for kids to play, yet kept up in a way where a good impression would be appreciated at business dinners.

While ringing the doorbell, I took in the atmosphere of the nearby fountain and the balanced design of the entryway. Frankly, I began to wonder why Elizabeth had called me in. As the door swung open, the voice on the phone matched the charm and humility now welcoming me in. It's not often that I take an instant liking to someone. With inner conviction, I knew in the first minute that Elizabeth and I would become longtime friends.

"Would you like me to show you around?" she asked nervously. It was the right question to ask. I love getting to know the house before I know the owner, even though I wasn't here to sell the house. "I have to apologize for the mess," she said in a lowered voice. Embarrassment hung on her childlike face.

Normally, messes don't bother me at all. I've seen everything when it comes to people's housekeeping. In some houses, the living room and kitchen are like sanctuaries while the rec room and kids' rooms look as though a tornado has hit. Some parents let their kids have free rein while others teach discipline at an early age. In some families one part of the house serves as a refuge for the miscellaneous and the scattered, usually to be found in the basement or storage area or garage. But in Elizabeth's house, clothes lay scattered in the upstairs bedrooms. Magazines and newspapers lay strewn about downstairs. *The house is a bit of a mess*, I thought. *She must have a wonderfully tolerant husband.* The tour continued.

"This is why I asked you to come," she said as if apologizing. "For some reason I am incapable of cleaning up messes. I have a housekeeper come in once a week but it really doesn't help. Within a few days it looks like this. No matter how hard I try, I'm not able to deal with clutter. That's why I decided to get personal help in resolving this problem. So I called you."

Tears brimmed on her eyelids. My heart went out to her. Her sincerity touched me in a way that stopped my breath. Experience has taught me that the last thing that will help people in situations like this is to try and change either the situation or the person. Patterns show up (repeated clutter) and traits of human behavior similarly present themselves because the patterns are supported and the traits held in place by some aspect of human consciousness. As Bruce Lipton points out, the culprit oftentimes rests within the subconscious. And we already know that the subconscious cannot be changed; it can only be replaced—and not by me but the one who created that subconscious in the first place. My desire to assist a person by trying to change their consciousness is like wishing Mohammed would come to the mountain. Sometimes the mountain has to come to Mohammed. And one cannot accomplish such a feat by desiring it so. One has to go talk to the mountain.

Talking to mountains is like listening to water: one has to understand the language, and oftentimes the language is that of symbols. That's why dreams are such a powerful tool in understanding what the subconscious mind is trying to get the conscious mind to pay attention to. Since boyhood, I have possessed an innate ability to work with symbols. As I grew into adulthood, I discovered what I call "dreamspeaking"—the ability to become the dream rather than analyze the dream.

I decided to tell Elizabeth about one of my most powerful tools in my medicine bag of tricks. It's called "holodynamics," conceived by Dr. Vernon Woolf, founder and director of the International Academy of Holodynamics, now located in Arizona. Dr. Woolf holds a doctorate in psychology (Child Development and Family Relations) and a bachelor's degree in physics. He based holodynamics on the principles of quantum physics—especially Bell's Theorem: "All of life is one"—and modern psychology. At the core of his work rests the notion that the mind and its levels of consciousness work like the rest of the universe: all facets, all levels, all compartments of the mind come forth from its source: Oneness. And like all aspects of the universe, these separations, these p-branes (dimensions), these compartments seek constant connection to that creative source.

Woolf created an ingenious method of replacing the subconscious by teaching facilitators, students, and clients how to regain access to the Oneness through the subconscious, thus allowing the subconscious to give up control to its creator so that a new and better subconscious could willingly come forth to alter reality. As a physicist, Woolf knew that the body contained trillions of microtubules that hold within them micro-black-holes. He came to realize that within our human bodies, we carry access to the very universe, which in and of itself contains monstrous black holes that operate in the exact same fashion as the miniatures—they are singularities. What are singularities? Gateways to Oneness. In his research, Dr. Woolf discovered that the human body, mind, and emotions could be refashioned from such Oneness.

I decided to take a weekend course with the good doctor and learn about holodynamics. What I came away with was a tool that I later adapted to my own language of the soul. As much as I admire the work of Woolf, as a man I found his patriarchal tendencies unsettling. Sometimes the inventor of a new discovery can be blind to its best purpose. Henry Ford's real genius was not in the creation of the Model T but in the creation of the assembly line. A similar comparison could be made with holodynamics: the real genius is not the technique but the fact that it can be so easily adapted, which means it's made to order in replacing the subconscious.

During my weekend course, I learned how to access the subconscious via a simple technique that takes the conscious mind into a trance state, or what Woolf calls the "place of peace." In my work, I've discovered more than holodynamics can work in this garden of opportunity. With holodynamics, the purpose is to call forth a holodyne. On his website, Woolf defines a holodyne as "a unit of cause." He continues:

> The world we experience as matter is held in place by holodynes that create quantum harmonics within our microtubules. These harmonics are sent as Frohlech frequencies coded with the information that controls the fine-grained and gross-grained (holographic) screens over all our senses. Our view of reality changes as these harmonics change. In other words, the experiences we have are controlled by our holodynes. The good news is that we can, as conscious beings, access and learn to manage our holodynes.

In more understandable terms, I take his viewpoint to mean that all of life is made up of consciousness. Arguably, everything that exists, exists because of consciousness. Like elementals, humans may attribute consciousness to anything, even an inanimate object or an abstract construct. Once the consciousness is attributed (think of this as zapping whatever you choose with consciousness, and poof, there it is) to any concept or object or thing, it then has the capacity to engage with your self, not unlike the Blue Fairy turning Pinocchio into a real boy.

What I find most remarkable about this technique is that it makes no difference if clients think they are making everything up or not, it still works. With many of my clients, once I tell them it's OK if they think they're making everything up, they relax and allow the holodyne to do its real work. And so it was with Elizabeth.

Once she allowed herself into her place of peace, she called forth the source of her inability to deal with messes. What showed up caused her words to catch in her throat. I had to encourage her to tell me what had shown up.

"It's Godzilla," she said as if the impossible had landed in her den. "Yeah, I keep thinking it's going to change but it doesn't. It's Godzilla." What I did not know was that she thought Godzilla represented her husband, and she did not want me to think her husband was a monster, so she began to do what I call editing.

"Great," I said, knowing full well she was trying to edit the holodyne. Such editing is not uncommon, oftentimes because the conscious mind does not want to deal with the realness behind the symbol. To edit a holodyne is to lose the power of its communication. If I don't encourage my clients in moments like this, I can lose the holodyne and thus the opportunity of engaging a new subconscious that later can alter the quantum reality.

"OK, how big is Godzilla?" This question I call the cement. If I can get the conscious mind to treat the holodyne as if it were a living thing, then the trance state holds and work can really begin.

"Well, it's Godzilla," she repeated as if asking me, Don't you get it? "It's huge."

What I like to do then is engage the emotions. "How does Godzilla feel about you?"

"Oh my God. He says he loves me."

This is a typical response from a holodyne. The holodyne, in actuality, is some aspect of the subconscious, usually trying to bring change to the person or a situation in which the person is stuck. The bottom line is that most of us love ourselves. We are creatures of love. We want the best for ourselves. Though this isn't always true in my work with clients,

I find that what comes in second place to love is peace. Either the holodyne loves us and wishes the best for us or it desires peace, sometimes at any cost, even if it means the ultimate cost—annihilation.

At this point in the journey, I began a second principle with Elizabeth that I use effectively with clients: dreamspeaking. For this to work, I, myself, had to become one with Godzilla. As a symbol, I could have seen Godzilla in a number of roles: destroyer, lizard (aggression), monster (ugliness), cartoon (absurd-based joy or laughter), or alien creature (aloneness or self-misunderstanding). Dreamspeaking avoids such analytical predispositions. By becoming Godzilla, I simply waited, hiding in his skin to see, hear, or understand what might be at the source of its creation. It didn't take long before I heard the word "mother." That told me what I needed to know.

With that piece of information, I was able to pose a number of questions that would allow Elizabeth to discover that Godzilla represented her personal power that yearned to break free from the chains that Mom had unknowingly placed on her. Mom was a caring woman whose life operated from fear: fear of doing the wrong thing, fear of pain, fear of loss, fear of loneliness. She wanted to protect her "Bethie" because her daughter meant everything to her. This resulted in a phenomenon I call "smothering mothering." And Elizabeth had been smothered to the point of revolt. Mom was a neat-freak, thus indicating that messes represented a revolt from the uptightness and strong control that Little Bethie had grown up with. The bottom line was that Elizabeth needed to feel her power, live in her power, use her power in a world that called her to be the gift she had been born to be. But Elizabeth's love for her mother burdened her with guilt at the thought of striking out on her own. Indeed, Godzilla was needed.

As beings of consciousness, holodynes, like elementals, can exist as long as we provide the consciousness and awareness to support that existence. Though holodynes are mere facets of the subconscious speaking to the conscious mind, the mind will interact with them as if they are caring beings here to help and support, thus providing a sense of environmental change around the self. The central factor in working with a holodyne is discovering what is it trying to accomplish and then find a better way (another holodyne—a companion, as it were) to support and accomplish the same end. In the case of Elizabeth, Godzilla was rebelling and revolting in an effort to break free and use its power. However, Godzilla might find a much better path to freedom and living in its power. To discover that, I asked Elizabeth to call in another holodyne that would allow her freedom and self-expression in a way that would serve her ultimate purpose as a human being. What showed up was a ball of light.

I asked Elizabeth to put Godzilla on hold while we dialogued with the ball of light. In that conversation, the ball of light reminded Elizabeth that she fully had the capability of owning her personal power; she just had to take the responsibility of expressing it. I could tell by the reaction on her face that this simple suggestion brought her discomfort. Overtly displaying her power, making herself heard, struck her as being arrogant, not humble. I had to sympathize because her sincere humility had already triggered my fondness for her. Yet, how was she to find self-satisfaction herself unless she was willing to set boundaries? And one of the first boundaries would have to be teaching her sons why it's important to clean up their own rooms. To accomplish that feat, she, herself, would have to set an example. For her to set that example, she would have to replace the subconscious with one that would not use messes as means to display her personal expression of freedom.

To ease her taking responsibility for operating in a new reality, I suggested that she ask help from the ball of light, learning the best way for her to own her personal power without coming across as arrogant or self-centered. That was the key. The holodyne made a few suggestions she could use to set boundaries around herself and at the same time to invite people in as long as they respected who she was, and did not violate her purpose as a gentle soul that wielded surprising power. Relief shone on her face. We now stood at the final stage.

Once two holodynes that may seem to have conflicting values recognize that each is seeking the same benefit, the same end for the client, then the final stage is to bring them into Oneness. Oneness is the mechanism for transformation of the subconscious into a new subconscious. By merging Godzilla with the ball of light, a new, transformed holodyne emerges. In most cases, the name of the holodyne also changes. However, in Elizabeth's case, she had already established a fondness for Godzilla and kept the name in spite of the fact that he now was surrounded with this great light.

Before I left, I gave Elizabeth homework to do to concretize the holodyne, the new subconscious. I also demonstrated how powerful Godzilla was by taking her through an exercise in which she had no strength when I tested one of her meridians—in her case the lung meridian, which represented her need to breathe in joy and life while speaking out her truth with a voice that now demanded to be heard. Then I asked her to have Godzilla clear the lung meridian and bring in any aspect of healing needed around past wounds. She watched curiously as Godzilla started expanding his light to the point where she saw and I felt it enter her lungs. There was a twinkle in her eye as she announced that Godzilla was done. I then retested her. She had full strength. Her mouth dropped open with the word, "Amazing." My work was done. Or so I thought.

As I hugged Elizabeth goodbye, I reiterated to her the homework I had given her and at the same time blessed her for the difficult work she had taken on in removing the blocks that had for so long ruled her life. Driving home, I realized I would miss her company, for she truly had done great work, which not all clients are willing to do. I laughed to myself thinking that she had created a holodyne named Godzilla, truly her alter-ego.

A few days later, Elizabeth called me again. Her husband, Ahmed, had noticed the difference in the house. Nervousness edged her voice as she told me that he was Egyptian, that he would like me to feng shui the house. Normally, I don't meet the husbands, usually because they are not on the same spiritual page as their wives and would rather not get involved with my work. What I would find out later was that he was in mortgage banking, transitioning into commercial real estate. He had heard from their mutual friend how I had worked with real estate agents. Should I meet with him? Hesitantly, I agreed. We set a date.

The fact that Ahmed was Egyptian brought back memories. A decade earlier, in my two trips to Egypt, I'd come to love not only Egyptian culture with its welcoming ways toward tourists, but also the Egyptian people. No matter where I chose to get lost (one of my favorite ways of really getting to know an area), the shop owners, the drivers, or the intelligentsia always invited me in for *shai* (tea) or meals. In spite of my phobia about drinking water the whole time I visited Egypt—tap water being undrinkable and bottled water containing magnesium to which I was allergic—I discovered that I could survive drinking chai. Anything else and I would spend the entire night on the toilet.

Personally, I find the Egyptian people magically warming. I remember my first trip where I discovered to my surprise their innate peacefulness, causing me to think, *No wonder they lost the wars, they are not a warlike people.* Years before, I had lived in Turkey when the Six-Day War started in June of 1967. My job was military intelligence, and I found Turks to be suspicious of all Americans. In some cases, downright hostile. I chose my travel destinations carefully, taking care never to travel alone. One day before I was scheduled to embark on a bus for my Holy Land vacation tour, the war broke out, and we were confined to the base. No military personnel were to leave. From my intelligence station, I watched the entire war unfold.

Visiting Egypt some twenty-five years later exposed me to a completely different perspective of its people. What I did not know about Ahmed was that he had grown up in Germany, and, frankly, his personality reflected far more German influence than his Egyptian roots. When he answered the door, I found myself stuttering at his tallness and his remarkable handsomeness. His eyes, though welcoming and bright, hid his serious German side. Elizabeth, of course, wrapped me in her endearing arms, gently ushering me into the living room, which appeared nearly spotless.

As Elizabeth headed off to the kitchen to pour me some water, Ahmed began peppering me with questions. They started out innocently enough. He expressed interest in how I used feng shui with realtors. To establish credibility with him, I confessed that no feng shui master would call what I do feng shui. The technique I used I called "personal feng shui," or "intuitive feng shui," in many ways different from traditional feng shui. I let him know that I referred clients who desired traditional feng shui to a colleague of mine who truly wore the mantle of feng shui master.

"It's the intuitive part that concerns me," he said, his eyes growing serious. "You helped my wife out a lot and provided a lot of information to her. You also provided a lot of information about my sons, who you have never met. Much of the information referred to their future. How is this different than fortunetelling?"

I knew where this was going. In my writing of *The Messengers*, I had faced many a fundamentalist trying to tell me that the angels I had written about were actually forms of Satan trying to trick people. In one section of the book, I had addressed the future that the angels said would be coming upon Earth. On radio talk shows, conservative evangelicals had called in to accuse me of using fortunetelling, strictly forbidden in the Bible. Having been to the seminary, I became adept in dealing with what I called "cherry picking" of Bible verses. I could hold my own. But the Quran I was not familiar with, though I did possess a copy and had read some passages as background for some of my writing.

"In Islam, fortunetelling is forbidden."

There it was. While at the seminary, I actually had studied historical "Mohammedanism," a Western term for what today is called Islam. Much to my surprise, I learned of the many similarities between Islam, Judaism, and Christianity. After leaving the seminary, I began to look at all religions as different facets of the same jewel. Rather than trying to make one right and the other wrong, I discovered they were like different languages. If one knew how to interpret from one language to the other, almost all differences could be seen as similarities.

I thought that Elizabeth had told me that Ahmed had majored in engineering while in college. So I decided to use my science background rather than my metaphysical background to explain what I did. As a mathematician, I learned a long time ago that if one looked at math as a language instead of a fog of numbers and formulas, the unintelligible and mysterious became greatly simplified. And that's how I worked with Ahmed, showing him demonstrations of quantum entanglement, tapping into what Jung called "group consciousness."

After explaining how dowsing rods really work with human consciousness and micro-movements, I could see the tension in him easing. Our conversation grew more personal and the exchange more friendly. He encouraged me to call him "Zak," a derivation of his last name. Midway into our conversation he asked me how I had acquired the mosaic of knowledge I had at my fingertips. I decided now was not the time to tell him about what I called "the library"—a special place of knowledge given to me by an angel after I had recovered from an incurable disease. Not even I fully understood the capacity or the full purpose of "the library." So I offered a history of my eclectic background that had brought both science and spirituality into the same camp.

"How did you know so much about my sons, Nuuh and Gibreel? It was actually kind of unsettling to hear how much you knew about them. How did you manage that?"

"It's not as difficult as it might sound," I said. "Even though I am particularly good at it, almost anyone can tap into what I do. Though some folks might call my ability to get information 'psychic' or 'clairvoyant,' really, it isn't. Almost all I do is based on what I call archetypal consciousness. All of life is holographic, which means it operates out of Oneness. And just like a hologram, you can see the whole from any single piece of the hologram."

I went on to explain how one can take a holographic plate and shine a laser through it, yielding a 3D image before you, similar to the scene in Star Wars where R2D2 produces an image of Princes Leia. If one changes the angle of the laser, the image appears to rotate or rearrange, showing a different 3D side to it. If one takes the holographic plate and throws it on a sidewalk, it shatters. Then, if a laser is directed through any shard, one still gets the same 3D image. It may not be as detailed but one still gets the image showing up.

I see life as a holographic plate. My plate is made up of archetypal systems. Some of the names given to these systems are Jungian archetypes, mythological archetypes, astrological archetypes, Freudian archetypes, I Ching archetypes, enneagram archetypes, etc. Even Islam has archetypes in its archangels and prophets. After going into detail as to how I use archetypes to gain information about my clients, I clarified for Zak that I had discovered within mathematics that any domain or mathematical system can be linked to, connected to, or converted to another domain or system through what is called a transformational matrix. Because I know this, I find similar ways to connect to any archetypal system a client may be operating under. Once I discover that,

I can then "transform" their system to one that works best for the situation facing my client. My job is to translate the language.

"In the case of your sons, my dowsing rods indicated that an angelic vibration or energy or presence was hanging out in Gibreel's bedroom. That tipped me off right away that I might be able to use what I call the angelic archetype to get information that would be useful to Elizabeth, who was worried about the happiness of her boys. I always pay attention when an angel shows up. I don't see them all the time but when I do or when I get a signal of one's presence, I know I'm supposed to engage with the angel to determine why it has made its existence known."

Zak wanted to know more about the angelic archetype and how I used it. I explained to him that in the book *The Masters Return*, which I co-authored with Joseph Crane, I give a great amount of detail on how the system works. I recommended he read it. Because of Zak's Islamic background, I decided to use a language that would be more in harmony with the language of the Quran.

"The angels taught us that there exists a system based on the number seven, which is considered a sacred number, even in mathematics. When our souls enter our bodies, they enter with light, or what I call a 'soul ray.' There are seven soul-ray colors that match the seven colors of the rainbow, ranging from red to orange to yellow, green, blue, indigo, and violet. In an appearance before Crane, the archangel Michael gave a number of traits that come in with each soul-ray color. When an archangel appears before a human, normally it carries one of these colors in its aura, or nimbus. That color is normally the opposite color of the human's soul ray. The reason for this is to bring balance to the person, to help the person. In the case of Gibreel, my rods told me that the angel in his room was Haniel, which carries the vibration of indigo in its nimbus. That told me that Gibreel's soul-ray color must be blue. Once I knew that, I was able to give Elizabeth a lot of information about Gibreel based on the archetype of the blue archangel, Ratziel."

I pondered whether my getting into the subject of angels might put off Zak. However, Islam, itself, has a rich angelic tradition. Curiosity framed Zak's demeanor as he began to pepper me with more and more questions, the final one being about his own soul-ray color.

I retrieved my dowsing rods from my medicine bag, as I like to call it, and asked him if he'd ever seen them operate, careful to avoid the term "water-witching." A broad smile wrapped across his face as I began to demonstrate how the rods worked. Immediately he asked if he could try them. That act alone told me legions about the man before me. He had gone from inquisitor to student in the matter of a conversation. That told me of the true depth of this man standing before me trying to get the rods to behave in his hands. After he was able to fumble an answer from then by finding the glass of water I had placed in the middle of the floor, I took them back to show him how I could determine his soul-ray color, which was red.

Reds are born leaders or holders of power. That explained Zak's aggressive approach when I first arrived. They also are trailblazers, inspiring others to follow, which also explained why he was not afraid to try the dowsing rods. Reds also can seem to be a bit arrogant when in truth they know the world operates around them. They're leaders. As long as a Red isn't caught in ego, they will not fall prey to arrogance. I let him know that as well. His big smile flashed back again. The more I conversed the more I realized what a gifted man he was.

Over the next couple of hours, both Zak and Elizabeth accompanied me as I made recommendations for the house based on my version of feng shui. Questions popped up often as we meandered from room to room. The dining room in particular carried wonderful energy, getting us into a discussion how any business meetings would bode well in such a room. Zak immediately confessed that past business dinners had proven fruitful. Now he knew why.

As the session ended, I realized I had made a new friend. Upon leaving, Zak let me know he was toying with the idea of selling the house. Would I come back to explore the house from that perspective if he decided to find a new home?

My defenses rose at this proposal as I thought about getting involved in real estate again. I let him know I would consider it. Of course, he wanted to know why my hesitation. A quick story of my past yielded a response, "You just weren't working with the right people. You should work with me."

I might have run in panic back to my car that very instant but the broad grin on his face enticed me to give one of my favorite answers: "Perhaps."

Months passed before I received another phone call from the princess that Elizabeth was. She and Ahmed had decided to sell the house. Would I come by to do my magic in getting it ready for sale. A long pause betrayed my worries about real estate again before I answered, "Of course." How could I not yield to charms of the delightful Elizabeth? Part of the reason for my wanting to say no stemmed from the collapse of the real estate market in Denver. Houses were not selling, and I didn't want to set up false expectations with my newfound friends. Nonetheless, my intuition told me nothing was predictable when it came to Zak. I would find out that my instincts were correct about him.

Within a week of clearing Elizabeth and Zak's house for sale, a buyer came forward. The sale had occurred so rapidly that they had to move into a rental. And this in a market where sales were far and few between. Impressed with the results, Zak asked me if I would work with him on his commercial real estate projects. Because of Elizabeth my frog had turned back into a prince.

KNOWING THE UNKNOWN

Zak continued to amaze me, becoming a chief example of what happens when belief systems fall to the unleashed forces of self-awareness. When he found new concepts and new ideas before him that tested his traditional upbringing, he did not build walls. He built bridges. He listened within to what called to him, even to the point of spending serious time and investment in studying Vedic astrology. The man who had challenged me as a possible fortuneteller was now himself using an archetypal system based upon the stars. To my marvel he did not stop there. He then dared to find a way of combining holodynes with astrology readings to create yet another archetypal system unique to the self-help world. At his invitation, I sat in on a couple of his sessions with clients and came to realize that Zak's real power as a Red was his ability to blaze new trails. The man was fearless.

In the angelic archetypal system, I am a Blue, or a teacher of wisdom. Blues love balance and justice in all things. They shine at showing others the gifts that lie within. And in so doing, Blues show others that by raising oneself up to one's fullness, not only is the individual served and blessed, but so are those all around that individual. The world becomes a better place because the quantum dictum that "All of life is one" truly applies to each individual. John Donne had it correct in his classic poem "For Whom the Bell Tolls":

No man is an island,
Entire of itself.
Each is a piece of the continent,
A part of the main.
If a clod be washed away by sea,
Europe is the less.

In the angelic archetypal system there exist subsystems, pairings. One of those pairings is called the "healing pairs." Blues and Reds happen to be one pairing. This same type of relationship exists between Greens and Indigos, Yellows and Oranges, Violets and other Violets (*The Masters Return*, Angel Gate Publishing, 2006, page 196). Individuals of these soul-ray colors, when paired together, have the ability to help others move into a place of self-healing. Zak's system of holodyne-based Vedic astrology reflected that pairing as he took systems that worked well for me and bridged them with systems that worked well for him. However, there is an interesting counterpart to this pairing. Blues and Reds naturally test one another, creating a kind of tension that forces the other into fullness. At times this tension can be contentious while at other times it's similar to the tension in the giant redwood (called turgor) that makes it possible for these giants to attain heights unmatched even today by modern architects.

Transfixed, I continued to observe Zak, continued to work with him. So determined had he become at discovering his fullness that I feared for his safety. Years have taught me not to try to change anyone. I can only offer advice when it is requested. To do otherwise is an affront to the other and a supreme waste of my time and gift. But Zak was like watching a car race, knowing full well the possibility that the lead car might crash against the retaining wall. You don't want any harm to come but there is nothing you can do, and you can't take your eyes off it.

Chapter 7

THE WAY OF WONDER OR
THE WANDERING WAY

In the movie *Excalibur*, Merlin tells King Arthur, "You and the land are one." This principle comes from one of the ancient paths during the time of Arthur, called the "Way of Wyrd." The word "weird" comes from this ancient belief system. Basically, the Wyrd operates on the belief that all of life connects via a web that communicates back our destiny, thus determining our fate. As with all belief systems, Arthur's fate is to end up being blinded by his own fears, his own self-made limits, which end up separating him from the land of Camelot.

Zak's pursuit of his own fate, his ever-pushing attempts to find enlightenment as quickly as possible, drove me to the edge of umbrage. In his rush, he convinced himself that I held the clues that would allow him to solve the mystery of who he was meant to be rather than trust in his own path, his own way of the wanderer. It's not that he exhibited ADHD like many of the Quantum Generation I had worked with, it's that as a trailblazer, he did not look at boulders on his path as challenges from which he might learn. Instead he saw such blocks as mandates that he find or make a new branch off the path. Working with him was like trying to track a pinball controlled by a pinball wizard.

The last straw came from a phone call in which he asked me what he could do to be more successful with his commercial real estate. He wanted to take the abilities he had seen in me and apply them to business, thinking it would give him an edge. What abilities might he learn in order to be a force in the boardroom so that success might sit at his feet?

I do have a temper. But I've learned to channel it in more constructive directions. So rather than deliver the lecture that was storming my mind, I gave him an alternative: "Meet me tomorrow morning in Fort Collins at a place called the Environmental Learning Center. I've given several workshops out there, so I know the area well. There's something I want you to see."

Of course he wanted details as to what I had in mind but I refused to divulge them. "Just meet me there." Because the directions were complicated, he decided to pick me up at my house. As we took the back roads to this hallowed spot monitored and stewarded by Colorado State University, I chose to say nothing, pointing when we needed to turn. As we waggled over the dirt road leading into the Environmental Learning Center (ELC), a large complex of buildings loomed across a canal on our left. Noticing Zak's curiosity, I decided to ask him, "What do you think those buildings are?"

"A warehouse? Sure stinks. Do they process garbage or something?"

"No," I answered, thinking this would be a good place to start with the lessons of the ELC. "It's actually a sewage-treatment plant. Most people would put their noses in the air, for reasons other than the smell, at such a thought of putting a waste-treatment plant next to an environmentally sensitive area, but this place is not what it seems. The wetlands of this area are part of the treatment process. Wetlands have amazing abilities to take pollutants out of water.[3] More and more cities are looking to wetlands as a replacement for chemical treatment. Colorado State University is working with the city of Fort Collins to bring nature and industry together. Quite something. This is a great example of creating harmony by working with the land."

Zak pursed his lips in that interesting-but-I-know-you-didn't-bring-me-here-for-this way of his. Off to our right appeared a lagoon, the

---

[3] *USA Today*, October 28, 2006

ducks and other waterfowl basking in the sun. At this point, I wanted to determine how much of the land Zak would notice, whether he'd see how the different ecosystems flowed together, and how humans were fitting in. Following his eyes, it seemed to me he was more interested in where we were going to park than anything else. Sure enough.

"Do we park over in this graveled area?"

I pointed where I wanted him to park, a spot close to the main trail. Cyclists emerged from the forest on a bike path that paralleled the hiking trail. Again, I was checking to see how much Zak was recognizing about the land use of the ELC.

After coating myself in Mexican vanilla to keep the mosquitoes from devouring me, I led the way uptrail to a tributary of the Poudre River, technically named Cache La Poudre River, French for "hide the powder." The name originated from an incident in the 1820s when French trappers found themselves trapped in a typical Colorado out-of-nowhere snowstorm. Needing to save themselves, the trappers buried their gunpowder along the banks of the river and headed for safety. The Poudre, as locals call it, is well known for its abundance of wild trout. Because water rights in Colorado are "for fightin'," the Poudre herself has been the center of many battles, nowadays in courtrooms. The area where she flows through the Environmental Learning Center once was sacred ground to Native tribes in the area. And I was about to show Zak why the area was considered so sacred.

"Let me know if you feel anything," I said as we gazed into the beautiful waters of the river.

"Like what?" Zak asked, wanting to know what I was up to.

"Just check your feelings or your body for any kind of sensations," I directed, trying not to give away that he was standing in the middle of a positive vortex. After he shrugged his shoulders, I had him walk back to the path and approach the river slowly, paying attention to any change in sensation.

"I'm not sure what you're after," he said approaching the riverbank, "but there seems to be a kind of buzz in the air here. I don't feel it back there," pointing to the trail. "Is that what you're talking about?"

"It is," I said with gratification. "This entire area is replete with geomagnetic phenomena, several of which I'll show you. The shamans of this region used these phenomena for sacred ceremony, for initiations, and for healing. It's also part of the reason why so many waterfowl migrate through here, some of them for breeding, others laying over on their way to South America and back. Powerful ley lines cross this part of Colorado, and whenever two ley lines cross, they create other phenomena like vortexes, power points, portals, and gateways. This is one of the few places in the world all these phenomena exist. It's why I have conducted several classes here over the years. My 'Voices of the Land' classes are among my most popular. Sometimes I'll have classes of up to forty people tip-toeing around here, learning about the different purposes of the Center as well as the Native traditions associated with the sacredness of the land."

"Show me more," Zak demanded. Rather than give him a lecture in appreciating where he was standing and learning from the land, I decided to wait. He followed me attentively as we approached a small suspension bridge straddling the Poudre. I didn't hesitate stepping onto the bridge, tromping onto the catwalk as if it were more trail. The swinging bridge always delighted me with its handmade appearance and its whimsical nature. I always tried to see how far I could get without having to grab onto one of the cables for support. With two people, the bridge gyrated like a miniature earthquake. I wanted to see what Zak's reaction would be. All I heard was laughter.

Native trees swallowed the trail on the other side. The 640-acre sanctuary is home to over seventy-five different varieties of trees, habitat for countless birds. Oftentimes the trails are crowded by bird watchers trying to spy a three-toed woodpecker or an osprey or a streak-backed oriole. On the southern edge of the Center rests the raptor rehabilitation project, home to many golden eagles, owls, and hawks that have been injured by power lines or reckless hunters.

The giant cottonwoods, hugged by Ponderosa pine, box-elder, Colorado spruce and fir, plunged the trail into deep shade as we wobbled off the rickety span of wood planks and cable. From experience, I knew the second phenomenon lay a short distance away. Deliberately slowing my pace, I waited to see if Zak would say anything. Nothing. As we trudged on, the trail turned sharply to the left following the edge of the river. Knowing that we would shortly enter the space of one of the largest negative vortexes I've ever seen, I decided to stop and prepare Zak.

"So you're not picking up anything?" I asked a bit disappointed.

"Well, now that you ask, I'm starting to get a little dizzy."

"Then why didn't you say something? I asked you to let me know if you felt anything."

"You're the teacher. Isn't it better for me to wait until you say something?"

"Not in this case. I've brought hundreds of people through these woods over the years. Some people have the ability of hearing the land and some don't. Even those who can't feel what you feel can be taught to use dowsing to pick up information. But this isn't about dowsing. It's about geomancy: the ability to read the land. There's no need to teach you the language of the land if you can't sense it."

Zak puzzled over the meaning of what I had just said. "Well, if that's the case, then we should go back a ways. I got a really heavy feeling after we left the bridge and entered the undergrowth."

"I wish you would have said something. That's exactly what you should have felt. Let's go back to that section, and stop me as soon as we enter it."

As we trekked back, we passed an area that I normally have classes check out because it has such a concentration of what are called nature spirits. However, I had already worked with Zak on an investment property in which the subject of devas came up. I decided to keep our conversation limited. Most people have a hard enough time trying to comprehend other worlds for the first time without my overwhelming them.

"Stop," he commanded. "It's here."

"Well done," I responded. "This part of the trail is one of the most powerful points on the reserve. What you are feeling right now is called a 'Hartmann line,' named after Dr. Ernst Hartmann, a German medical doctor who discovered that certain magnetic fields could interfere with the normal functioning of cells and nerves, thereby causing disease. Originally, he thought they were solely connected to the Earth's magnetic field. But others since then have discovered that these lines can also be created by power lines or radio stations or cell phone towers. Others, like myself, have found that these lines can also be created by events of high negative emotion, like an Indian massacre. Whenever I have found a Hartmann line running through a house, the couple had either ended up divorced or was in the process of divorce. These lines make me sick. I can only stand here for a minute or so. Time's up. Let's move on."

"Wait, wait," Zak chuckled. "You just can't walk away. I've got questions."

"I'll answer them when we've rounded the bend." After we turned left again, I stopped where we had rested before. Pointing into the trees, I said, "The line goes off straight into the woods. It doesn't go far. Hartmann lines aren't like ley lines in that regard."

"What do you do when you discover one?"

"I try to leave them alone. They exist for a reason. I've never messed with one here on the path because it holds the vibration, or the consciousness, of a traumatic event that has yet to be balanced. My guess is that a hunting party of some kind violated the sacredness of this area, probably killing someone or some thing. Because the line is so strong, my guess is that there was a group of people who were killed here. At one time, there stood a Council Tree here, which meant that any tribes could come together to meet, to air their differences, to make agreements, to powwow. Warring was never allowed here. That's the beauty of Council Trees, which were revered in Native spirituality. I'll show you the tree after I tell you a story that I want you to hear. But you must not let anyone know where the tree is. You'll see why later.

"Fort Collins has an interesting history along the Poudre. The Sioux, the Cheyenne, and the Arapaho hunted in this area, the Arapaho especially. They considered this land ceremonial, sacred, for the very reasons that find us here today. The Spaniards first opened the area because of gold. Then the Oregon Trail and the Santa Fe Trail brought the White Man. A branch off the Santa Fe Trail, called the Cherokee Trail, went right through here to California. In fact the Overland Trail stagecoach had a station right on this property. Lots of skirmishes resulted as treaties took over, displacing most of the Native peoples. That's why I believe there are so many Hartmann lines in this area."

When I have cases where a Hartmann line is causing trouble on a client's piece of property or in a client's house, then I take measures.

Otherwise, I am most careful when instigating any changes with the land. What Colorado State University is doing at the Environmental Learning Center is remarkable. They are restoring native plants and bushes, allowing wildlife to return and flourish. I've watched the students and volunteers do amazing work through the years, restoring parts of the land to its natural wonder and its sacredness. But there still remains the violent history that desecrated once hallowed land and cloaked the Council Tree where none would find it until the land once again vibrated with harmony.

If I'd let him, Zak would have spent the rest of the day hitting me with questions. I knew he had a business meeting in a few hours, so I decided to move him on to the next section of the trail. There was much I wanted him to comprehend before leaving the land. Past experience had taught me that the only way to make a lasting impression on him was to make a big impression. Otherwise I would be doomed to revisit past lessons with him repeatedly—and I'm not a patient man. Wasting time is not something I tolerate well.

As the trail opened up to clear sky, a large gravel bar loomed to the left. Though I had seen the river flood several times during the spring runoffs, the gravel bar shifted little, it was that big. I stopped where a small deer path led from the trail to the bar. Right away an old sensation from this spot returned. I knew I couldn't stand here long.

"Rather than tell you about this area," I started, "I'd like you to tell me yourself what you sense, pick up, or feel. I'd like you to follow this path out to the gravel bar. Stop where you think the sensation is the strongest, if you feel any sensation. OK?"

As usual, Zak wanted more detail but I refused it, directing him to proceed on his own, trusting his own instincts. Warily he waded through the tall grass until wet, soft sand forced him to tiptoe onto the gravel bar. After pacing another ten feet, he started to teeter. He beamed his surprise as he turned toward me. "I'm getting dizzy," he announced, as if anticipating I'd give him a reason.

"To be expected," I noted. "But continue until the dizziness reaches a peak and then let me know."

He returned to exploring, steadying himself as he proceeded another fifteen feet, stopping, coming back around, crisscrossing the center of the gravel bar. "This is the strongest point," he yelled. "Really weird. What is it?"

"Just stand there for another minute and try and get a bearing on what is happening in that spot. Then I'll tell you what it is."

While spreading his arms out as if on a high-wire, Zak turned in a circle, exploring the smooth stones and boulders that surrounded him. He stopped with a puzzled look and turned to me. "If feels like something is swirling around me."

"Excellent." I was pleased. "Which direction is it turning? Clockwise or counterclockwise?"

Once again he spread his arms out. "Counterclockwise, I think."

"What you're standing in is called a negative vortex. I can't even stand in them myself. They make me so weak I start to throw up."

"So why am I standing here?" Zak felt like a lab rat.

"You seem to be handling it well. But I wouldn't stay there much longer."

"What's it do?"

"Negative vortexes occur where two ley lines cross, one positive and one negative. If the stronger ley line is magnetic in nature, then the vortex swirls counterclockwise and is negative. If the stronger ley line is electric in nature, then the reverse."

I noticed another visitor crossing the bridge in the distance. I decided to hurry with my explanation. "Negative vortexes are used by Mother Nature to clean up areas energetically. Deer love to lie in them. Oftentimes you will find deer beds in negative vortexes. That's why this deer path is here. A few people flourish in negative vortexes. These people tend to have a lot of energy, too much energy. This kind of vortex helps balance them. However, most people get weak standing in them. The magnetic ley line—or negative ley line—moves south of you, across the river and not far from where we parked. Look at the trees along that bearing and tell me what you notice."

Zak turned, also spotting the advancing visitor, and scanned the trees. "They look like they're leaning. Is that what you're talking about?"

"Exactly. That's how I find these phenomena—by watching the trees. Most trees bend toward the south where the sun travels across the sky.

But the trees along the ley line bend inward, east and west toward the ley line. Come on out of there before I have to come and get you."

Zak wobbled back to the main trail. I politely said hi to the hiker as she passed us.

"Wow, that was something," Zak enthused. "I didn't even know I could detect such things. Can anybody feel these?"

"No. I'd say about forty percent of people in my classes can sense these phenomena, and another forty percent can pick them up with dowsing. The remaining twenty percent think the whole bunch of us are crazy. Come on. Time is fleeting. Let's go to the next area."

Upon reaching the main branch of the river some hundred feet later, I had Zak follow me over rocks to an outcropping close to the flow of the stream. This would be the part that I wanted him to pay particular attention to. As we sat down, I reviewed part of what I had wanted him to recognize. "My reason for bringing you here is to teach you to pay attention to the land. You sell land, you buy land. Your life depends on the land. Yet how often do you really pay attention to the land? If you more fully participate in how you exchange land and why you exchange it, you will do much better financially with your efforts. Mother Nature by design is meant to assist us, support us, comfort us. But how do we repay her? Mostly with ignorance. If you can learn to pay attention to the language of the land, then you will be able to pay much closer attention to what really happens in the office. Our bodies are made from the land: 'Dust thou art and to dust thou shalt return.' Like the land, our bodies speak a similar language that few pay attention to. Some call it 'body language,' but that's a subset of the complete language.

"What I am going to teach you now comes from an ancient spiritual tradition called the 'Way of Wyrd.' I have updated it, using the principles of quantum entanglement and holodynes into a system I call the 'Way of One.' I first became aware of the Way of Wyrd through a fictional book called *The Way of Wyrd*, by Brian Bates (Hay House, 2005)." Summarizing the book, I told Zak about some of the philosophies Bates had drawn upon in writing the book. Bates had discovered an ancient text preserved in the vaults of the British Library, written about a thousand years ago, which he describes as follows:

That manuscript is a handbook of healing remedies, sacred ceremonies, and spiritual secrets of an indigenous shaman of ancient England—teachings for today from our ancient past. It became the touchstone for all of my research.

It showed that at the heart of Anglo-Saxon spirituality is the experience of 'wyrd'. Today, the term 'weird' means something strange, bizarre, or supernatural. But in its archaic and original sense, it meant that aspect of life which was so deep, so all-pervasive, and so central to our understanding of ourselves and our world, that it was inexpressible.

Stemming from this essential vision, our Anglo-Saxon ancestors believed in a universe where lines of power ran through the earth, spirits inhabited the trees, streams and stones, and where magicians were able to look into the future through the mysterious power of runes. People understood their universe as held together by an interlaced web of golden threads visible only to the wizards.

I conveyed to Zak how much of the Wyrd explained many of my own experiences with nature, especially the information taught to me by a shaman-priest from Africa, Malidoma Somé, with whom I studied for a year. It was Malidoma who awakened in me abilities that resonated with the forces of Nature. From his upbringing, Malidoma learned the tradition of the Dagara, an African tribe in the regions of Burkina Faso, Ghana, and the Ivory Coast, that held Nature as a supreme force, not unlike our notion of God, where the separation between natural and supernatural did not exist. Malidoma's influence caused me to learn the language of the Stone People as well as the Tree People and the nature spirits. When I discovered the strong similarity between the African tradition and the Anglo-Saxon tradition of the Wyrd, I began to explore more fully how these traditions also paralleled what I had learned about the angelic realms. From all that, I began to formulate what I call the "Way of One," which I now explained to Zak.

"Like the Way of Wyrd, the Way of One rests on the quantum physics principle (Bell's Theorem) that all of life is connected. All of life is here to help us, to support us. We just have to learn how to see that. I see the land and all it nurtures as a hologram of information. If we pay close attention to the details, oftentimes we can connect to the bigger picture. I'd like to take you through a few exercises to illustrate that. Find a comfortable spot to sit next to the river."

"This isn't going to hurt, is it?" Zak asked with a grin, finding himself a smooth rock on which to plant himself.

"Only if you want it to," I answered, wondering whether I ought to cancel the lesson until he could take it seriously. "The first component of entering the Way of One is through intent. In Lynn McTaggart's book, *The Intention Experiment: Using Your Thoughts to Change Your Life and the World* (Free Press, 2007), she describes a series of lab experiments conducted by Dr. William Tiller, featured in the movie, *What the Bleep Do We Know!?*"

Tiller, professor emeritus of materials science and engineering at Stanford University, created a set of legendary experiments where he tested whether intention (thoughts) could affect a chemical process. In his experiments, he placed intention into a "black box," an electronic device, by having himself and a few colleagues enter into a meditative state. Tiller would then read the intention aloud, having everyone then hold the intention into the black box for fifteen minutes. In his most surprising experiments, the intention was to shift the pH of water one full unit on the pH scale. The significance of this range of change in nature would be considered unthinkable. McTaggart cites an example that if the pH in a person's blood changed even half a pH unit, up or down, that would be enough to kill the person. After imprinting the black boxes with the intention, Tiller would then wrap the black boxes in aluminum foil to block any outside influence and then ship them 2,000 miles away to another lab where the black boxes would be unpacked and set next to pH-neutral water. To their delight, within a few days the pH of the water changed a full pH unit. The implications were extraordinary. This was scientific proof that human consciousness could alter physical reality.

As Tiller's team continued to replicate the experiments in an effort to comprehend what they had discovered, they noticed that the temperature in the lab began to increase. No matter what they did to try to bring the temperature back down to normal, it continued to increase as the number of experiments increased. Eventually, they had to close the lab and start a new lab at a new location. But to their chagrin, the same phenomenon occurred all over again. What they later discovered was that the intention experiments were creating a Bose-Einstein condensate state (a higher state of coherence) which was transforming the entire lab into a state of oneness.

Rightly so, Zak had several questions as to what is intention. I instructed him to think of a question to which he needed an answer, and then hold that thought for five minutes. While he held the question in his mind, I also asked him to scan everything around him, paying close attention to all detail with regard to nature: listen, smell, see, feel, and hear. Everything.

"Do you want me to tell you the question?" he asked, finally getting interested in what was about to unfold.

"No. Not now. Wait until I'm ready to explain the consequences to you."

For five minutes Zak paid attention to everything around him as did I. Having done this exercise many times, I immediately paid attention to which direction the wind was blowing, watching for any bird, listening for any calls from animals, counting every fly, beetle, bird, or human that came into our area.

Once the five minutes was up, I asked Zak what he had noticed. He looked at me as if he were taking a test that he knew he was about to fail. "Well, the river flowed by beautifully. Is that what you're talking about?"

"Anything else?"

"Uhh. The mosquitoes are driving me crazy."

"Did you hear the train in the distance?"

"No."

"Did you see the fish surface on the river?"

"No."

"Did you count how many birds flew overhead?"

"No."

"How about the cloud of gnats that flew in front of you?"

"I think you know the answer," he mumbled, hanging his head.

"Zak, this is all important. Numbers reveal patterns. For instance, the five crows that flew overhead are showing the number for change. Five is the number of change in one's life, while eight is the number for change in one's destiny. Three is the number of balance, two the number of duality, four the number of stability, six the coming together of opposites or the indicator of health conditions, seven the number of consciousness or divine timing, nine the number of fulfillment or gestation. Crows are symbols of messengers or a message being given to you, usually a warning."

"How do you expect me to know all this?"

"I don't. But what I do expect is for you to listen to what I'm trying to tell you. You've asked me to show you how I do what I do. You want to bring it into your business, into the boardroom, where you can discern and decide what will serve you best. Let's try this again. We'll take another five minutes. This time, really pay attention." I gave him my bottle of Mexican vanilla to help keep the mosquitoes away, even though the wind was picking up, which would eventually drive them away.

Once again, we sat in silence, this time locking in to everything around us. When five minutes had expired, I turned to him. "Well, what did you notice?"

He went down his list of observations. I smiled.

"Did you see the red-tailed hawk?" I asked.

"No, but I heard what I thought was a hawk. Where was it?"

"Just over the tree tops." I pointed to the northeast section of the land. "Do you know what a hawk stands for?"

"Isn't it the symbol of Horus?"

"That's the falcon, which has shown up around you on a couple of unexpected occasions. The hawk symbolizes courage, the kind of courage that allows one to see from on high. This should give you the first clue to your question. The fact that you didn't see it indicates that you are blind to the big picture, the overview. Let's look at your question, your intention now."

"I asked to be shown what I ought to do about this business deal I'm thinking of making."

"OK, let's start with the birds. How many did you see?"

"I saw eight birds."

"Do you know what kind they were?"

"No."

"Two were swallows, two were finches, two were starlings, and two were oriels—I think. The point is that they always showed up in pairs. That indicates to me that you should not enter into this business arrangement alone. You need a partner who will look out for your best interest. Did you notice the direction most of the birds were flying?"

"Uh, that way." He pointed north.

"Yes, that's the north. The north symbolizes wisdom, the kind of wisdom that safeguards against ignorance. This is a warning to you about this guy you are thinking of partnering with. He has not used wisdom, which means you should. Look into the details of what he is proposing. Rid yourself of the ignorance that he has fallen to. The south represents pursuit of spiritual consciousness or awareness or yearning for growth. The west signifies the union between light and darkness, or death of the old, while east stands for rebirth, the rising sun of spiritual ascendance or growth. The minor directions represent a combination of the directions they straddle."

Knowing he had left it off his list, I asked, "How many people did you notice come by?"

"One. From back on the trail."

"Male or female?"

"I don't know."

"Male. Alone. His eyes were on the trail as he was running, not looking around. This is you. You think you are entering into a situation that will involve a partner, but in truth you will find yourself alone because you aren't looking around, seeing the big picture."

We then talked about the number of insects, usually an indication of how small detail can get in the way or bug a person. Zak didn't see the mayfly, an indication of short life, but he did see the two bees, which I had missed. Once he pointed out to me where they were and what they were doing, I realized they symbolized his need to busy himself with another project other than the one he asked about in his intent. He needed to find himself a true business partner, not one that mostly wanted Zak's financial backing.

A look of exasperation crossed his face. "How can I ever learn how to do this Way of One? There's no way I can know what you know, or can do what you do. No one can."

"Not true," I countered. "I've studied symbols and numbers and meanings for years, many years. I will give you a list of books to start with, like the *Dictionary of Symbols*, Tony Crisp's *Do You Dream?*, Joseph Campbell's *The Power of Myth*. These are great starting places. Don't expect to understand the Way of One overnight. It will take years. And you are a fast learner. If you really want to take what I do into your business meetings, start simply. Instead of reading the land, learn to read bodies, eyes, posture, words avoided and words overused. It's the same principle. I can sit in a business meeting and watch the eyes of the people across from me. If a person's eyes are looking to the left, that indicates they are using the right brain, or the intuitive side, which can tell me they are guessing. If their eyes move to the right, that's the analytical side. If their eyes are pointing down, they are usually hiding something. If their eyes look up, they are hopeful. If their chair is pointed right at me, chances are they are truthfully engaging me. If the chair is pointed away at an angle, there is something they are trying to avoid. All of this is part of the Way of One. All aspects of life indicate the truths we seek. In statistics there is a law that states, 'Any single event can predict the whole.' This is statistics' version of the Way of One."

We live in a world of the instantaneous, where information from across the world and around the globe is at our fingertips. The technology of the Internet has blessed us with access to tremendous bodies of data, but it has also made us lazy to the pursuit of the ways of wisdom and the discovery of spiritual realms beyond computers and high-tech gadgets. These realms can only be acquired by decades of study and miles of patient experience.

"Before we go to the hidden Council Tree, there is a story I wish to tell you. Let's head off that way while I tell it."

THE STORY OF THE LAND AND DEATH

Years ago, a mother called me, telling me her son was dying. Would I help? She had taken him to all kinds of doctors and none of them could find anything wrong. Yet the son grew worse. The mother was bereft, grieving as she watched her boy slowing wasting away, now at death's feet. I asked her why she thought I could help. My reputation had spread, and with the spreading were claims I, myself, would have never made. This is what happens when people do not claim their own power and recognize that they are the source of their own healing. My job is simply to remind them of that power. It does not do future clients or me any good to create myth and exaggeration about my role.

When I asked how old her son was, she replied that he was twenty-four. She was not cheered by my response that since he was an adult, her son would have to ask me himself. As goodhearted as the mother was, I have found that only one person matters when it comes to healing work, and that is the person in need of finding healing. I also told her that her son would have to make a donation for any work I did. That I would accept no donations from her. This also did not please her. Her son had not been able to hold a job from the time he was sixteen. She told me that at that age he had undergone a serious heart surgery. The surgeons had to electrocute part of his heart tissue. Ever since then he had experienced nothing but problems. Nonetheless, I let her know that no matter how small the donation, the son was the one who had to offer it.

With my work, I find this donating to be a key indicator as to where clients are in their attitude about investing in themselves. They need to see themselves as valuable and capable of receiving by being able to give in return as a fair exchange. The reason behind this is that many people simply do not see themselves worthy of blessing or wellness or hope, deserving only crumbs from the table of life. Consequently, with beggar mentality, they also see themselves as too poor to give. It was a hard lesson for me to learn that people often live by the adage "Pay nothing, worth nothing."

My history shows that the person being represented by the well-wisher most often does not call back. Yet two days later, I heard from the son. I will call him Jake to honor his privacy, for it is a strange tale that ensued.

His first confession melted my heart. "I'm afraid I'm going to die." He wept openly.

The first thing I had to do was calm him, give him hope. Over the phone I went through a number of questions to determine how dire his situation actually was. Everything he ate he either threw up or voided within minutes. His body was rejecting food. I told him that I had a technique for getting the body to become less sensitive to allergies. My own bout with food allergies made me particularly aware how devastating they can be. At one point the technician studying my allergies told me that I was the first person she'd ever seen who was allergic to eating. The only way I found relief was through alternative care from a legend in the Fort Collins area, Gloria Green. From her I realized a whole new world existed between the limited confines we perceive as the human body and the unlimitedness of human consciousness. So I had a good idea what Jake might be going through. Until I arrived, I asked him to drink only liquid broths. He acknowledged that he was able to keep beef broth down. After determining that he couldn't make it out his mother's front door, let alone drive, I made an appointment to visit him the next day.

As soon as I stepped into the house, my head started reverberating. After greeting Jake and his mother, I let them know that I'd like to check out the premises, that I was getting signals that something unusual lurked in the house. As I walked the two floors of the house, and then the grounds, two phenomena stood out. The first was a strong negative vortex in the house, particularly noticeable in the basement. Most people can't live in a house with a negative vortex. Oftentimes what I do is either shut it down or move it, if I am allowed. In rare cases my rods tell me it must be left alone. And this was one of those cases. That told me that those in the house were either high-energy people or insensate. It didn't take me long to figure out that both Jake and his mother had the energy of a buzz saw.

The second phenomenon was the presence of an angry old woman hanging around Jake. Normally, I don't see spirits. I can feel their presence and dowse their presence but I normally don't see them. When I do, I know I'm supposed to do something about their indwelling. Past apparitions have taught me that I don't say anything to the client about this unless I must. People will immediately jump to the conclusion that they are being haunted or possessed, when neither is the case.

A mystery stood before me. Do I tackle the old woman, or figure out what to do about the vortex? I decided to address both. In the past, I discovered that any kind of negative presence, whether elemental or spirit, will not enter an angelic gateway. If any negative consciousness tries to enter an angelic gateway, either the gateway will shut down, or it will repel the consciousness. With this in mind, I constructed an angelic gateway in the basement (*The Masters Return*, Angel Gate Publishing, 2006, page 23) where the negative vortex was at its strongest. Angelic gateways themselves create vortexes within them, two in fact. The actual energetic makeup of these gateways is based upon pyramid geometry. One square pyramid sits right side up with a vortex spinning counter-clockwise while the second pyramidal structure is upside down with a vortex spinning clockwise into the earth. By collapsing the geometry from 3D to 2D, one has an angelic gateway.

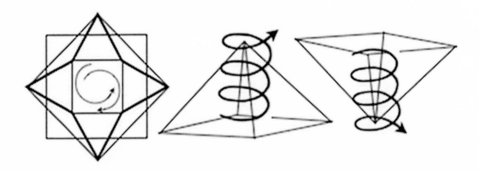

Through the years, I discovered that the gateway does not interfere with natural vortexes but, in fact, enhances them. Interestingly, even though a gateway can enhance a negative vortex, the gateway will not support any kind of negative consciousness within it.

I then placed Jake in the middle of the gateway. The old woman hung outside the geometry of stones. This told me what I needed to know. First, that this presence was not supposed to be hanging around Jake, and second, it didn't intend to leave. It would wait until Jake left the safety of the gate to continue its purpose. I now knew I had to discover that purpose. After ten minutes, Jake reported feeling better. After another twenty minutes the nausea and the burning in his eyes ceased.

As Jake improved, I decided to see if I could work with his body like I had worked with the land. There is a technique where one can get the body to tolerate the vibration of a food that is creating an allergy. I asked Jake what food normally sustained him the best, what get him through the day. His response was rice and chicken or beef.

Years ago a good friend gave me a wonderful book (no longer in print) written by Peter Aziz, a shaman out of England. When I devoured the book, *Working with the Tree Spirits in Shamanic Healing* (Counter Culture, 1994), I realized I had a powerful tool in working with acupuncture meridians. Years before receiving the book, the angels had given us a technique to clear Chinese meridians using tuning forks and sacred oils. As amazing as it was to learn the connection between the angelic realm and Chinese meridians, it also took forever. One used a detailed chart that mapped the meridians onto the body inch-by-inch and assigned numbers to each acupuncture point. Aziz's book gave me a technique to discover when a meridian was blocked, and critical points on the meridian that could be used to clear it. Instead of taking hours to assist a client, it now took minutes. And in many cases proved more effective than needles.

Another colleague and great friend, Cheryl Rennels,[4] exposed me to the work of Dr. Robert Frost,[5] who created a system for working with the meridians to desensitize the body's reaction to foods, allergens, or compounds. The technique is surprisingly simple. First, make sure a meridian is clear. Then place a suspicious food, allergen, or compound into a plastic baggie and station it over the belly button (lower dan ti'an). If the cleared meridian shows evidence of blockage, you know you have an allergy at work. If you keep the plastic baggie in place, and clear any

---

[4] www.WeBlessYourHeart.com

[5] www.JoyousWorld.com

and all meridians blocked by the allergen, you get the body to harmonize with the substance instead of fight with it. Normally, I have clients wait until the next morning before trying small amounts of the problem food. However, much to my horror, I have had clients who didn't wait, and after only fifteen minutes swallowed food that normally would have put them in the emergency room. Not recommended. Be careful and take your time. We are all different.

After about half an hour, I had Jake cleared of his reaction to rice, chicken, and roast beef. The next day would tell the tale. And it did. As long as someone kept clearing his meridians using Dr. Frost's technique, he was carefully able to eat again. But what about the old woman?

My next effort consisted of using a holodyne to find out what the old woman represented. What came forth were indicators that Jake was at war with himself. His whole life had been a struggle since the heart surgery, and like many Quantum Kids, deep inside he wanted to destroy the world that had nearly destroyed him. So deep and abiding was his anger that he felt afraid to show it or display it. The ultimate reason why these young people want to destroy our world is that they believe destruction, and that alone, will bring peace. Ultimately, peace is all they actually want. His repressed anger left him vulnerable to this being of consciousness who fed on anger. I knew it might take years for Jake to deal with this magnitude of anger. But he had only days, not years. I had to find a way to keep the old woman from feeding off of him, creating scenes that fostered further anger. So great had been Jake's outbursts that, at one point, Jake's mom confessed that she had, on occasion, feared for her life. My strategy was to engage him, showing him with holodynes that peace was possible in better ways. Destruction was not the most effective remedy in finding peace. Once he saw that, his repressed anger had an alternate path to escape. But I had to keep the old woman away until he came to peace with himself.

During one angelic apparition with Joseph Crane, the angels disclosed that another tool existed to keep away negativity. Pendants and jewelry with specific geometry could be worn to protect from any onslaught of negativity. The geometry had the same shape and number of stones as the angelic gateway. In what they called the Gate of Light, the violet stone (charoite) used in the angelic gateway was replaced with another semi-precious crystal called tanzanite. I decided to create a Gate of Light over Jake's headboard so that he could sleep through the night and work on his computer in his room without the presence of the old woman. It worked.

Over a period of years Jake learned how to work with the land and the patterns of life to bring his own life back into balance. On a number of occasions he would end up in the emergency room with doctors still unable to find a thing wrong with him other than finding him severely dehydrated. This was in spite of his drinking copious amounts of water. Dr. Robert Frost's work on a little known factor in the body called "ground substance" eventually gave Jake another tool to keep his body grounded where it could absorb water.

As Jake's health grew, so did his abilities. It didn't take long before he could detect the presence of the old woman. Shortly after that, he sent her away, never to return. With most of my clients I have found that the fear of the unknown is far worse than dealing with the fear. Such was the case with Jake. Once he realize that he possessed the power to decide who entered his space, he no longer saw himself as a victim. He has become one of the most extraordinarily gifted people I have met. Someday I will tell you further unbelievable tales of this light among the Quantum Generation. What Jake now represents is a doorway to unknown worlds, instead of a crusader trying to destroy our own world.

THE COUNCIL TREE

"I don't get it," Zak said. "Why are you telling me this story?"

"Are you or are you not a servant of the land?"

"If you mean do I make my living with it, the answer is yes. I thought we had established that."

"But what do you know about the land?"

"I know how to buy it and sell it. You think I should know more?"

We had hiked to a heavily wooded section of the trail where several trees lay flattened on the ground. A small trail led into a hidden glen. It was there we stopped.

"Tell me what you see," I said. Zak gave me a look like someone who had walked into a classroom only to discover the teacher had sprung a pop quiz. His eyes began searching, seeing little.

"What am I supposed to see?" he asked, giving up. His rich black hair waved with the breeze. He folded his arms as if daring the land to touch him with its secrets.

"The Council Tree," I replied, waiting to get his reaction. Combing his fingers through his hair, once again he searched the glen seeing nothing of importance.

"Where?"

Knowing time was growing short, I pointed to the sacred tree about fifty feet away.

"What? That dead thing?"

I chuckled, wondering if it might be better to simply leave now, rather than spend any more time trying to get him to understand the land. "So you think it is dead? Go stand next to it. Sometimes things are not what they seem." Across the glen stood the remnants of the once mighty symbol of peace, a huge cottonwood some twelve feet in circumference. A trail of burned bark and black xylem revealed that the majestic edifice had met its demise from a great lightning bolt. Only leafless, broken branches remained, many of them decaying in the soil. Zak stood next to it.

"I'm getting dizzy again. What's going on?"

"Do you remember the last time you had that feeling?"

"Yes, over by the river bank where the positive vortex was. Is this also a positive vortex?"

"More than that," I said. "About a hundred feet to your left is another vortex, a negative vortex, similar to the one we just left, only this one isn't quite as big or as strong. Whenever a positive and negative vortex are close together, they form a natural gateway. If you step to your left about ten feet, you'll be in the gateway."

"Can I go through it?" he asked with that kidlike grin of his, as if he were at an amusement park about to enter the fun house.

"That depends," I said.

"On what?" he asked as he stepped under a tree whose limbs gnarled in a circular fashion around him.

"On whether you have eyes to see. You didn't notice the Council Tree. You thought it dead even though it continues to buzz with a life that ordinary eyes can't see. The First Nations of Colorado considered the large cottonwoods special and sacred, calling them 'Standing Nation.' Lame Deer, a Lakota holy man was famous for noting that the leaves of the cottonwood are shaped like a heart. To this day, the cottonwood is used at the sacred Sundance initiations. Black Elk, an Oglala Sioux medicine man, used the cottonwood as a symbol when talking about his people."

One of his famous quotes is applicable to the Council Tree:

I saw that the sacred circle of my people was one of many circles, that all together made one circle.... and in the center grew one mighty flowering tree to shelter all the children of one mother and father. I saw that it was holy.

It is a very tall tree with rustling leaves, and the animals and people mingled like relatives. It was filled with singing birds.

I heard the wind blowing gently through the tree and singing there. The Sacred Pipe came on eagle wings from the east and stopped beneath the tree, spreading Peace around it.

In the book, *Black Elk Speaks*, by John Neihardt (State University of New York Press, 2008), we find a defining statement that is relative to the Environmental Learning Center:

... the Grandfathers had shown me my people walking on the black road and how the nation's hoop would be broken and the flowering tree be withered, before I should bring the hoop together with the power that was given me, and make the holy tree to flower in the center and find the red road again.

I said to Zak, "When the sacredness of this spot was defiled by those who waged war, the tree spirit withdrew. That's why it appears dead. But it is far from dead. The day has come when peace will once again reign over this land. If you look closely, you will see a shoot rising out of one of the old roots."

Zak stood in the gateway holding his hands out, his eyes closed. Finally, he seemed to be understanding how hallowed this place was. He was seeing.

After he lowered his arms, I asked him once again, "Tell me what you see. Pay attention to all the other trees."

Surprisingly, he took his time. "There seem to be a lot of dead trees around here. Is that what you mean?"

"Yes. Well done. Notice how so many have fallen to the land. Do you remember seeing this anywhere else along the trail?" He had not. It was as if bursts of past winds had paid special attention to this part of the land, and the trees had given up their lives in honor of the sacredness of this spot, bowing upon the land.

"Notice how there is a natural amphitheater here. I believe this is where the First Nations met in peace to iron out their differences and powwow. It's as if the fallen trees could serve as pews. Anytime I have found a natural gateway in a wooded area, I've seen this kind of treefall, where the surrounding trees appear wanting to let the forest know that sacredness is near. The other indicator I always find near a natural gateway is what I call the guardian plant-spirit. It's an unusual plant or bush or tree that grows only near the gateway and nowhere else in the immediate ecosystem. Can you find it?"

Zak appeared bewildered by all that he could not see. Whenever we closely look at nature we find entire worlds exist that heretofore seemed invisible to us. A dear friend of mine, a dedicated biologist, made me aware of this invisibility of nature. She once took me to a drainage ditch and sat me next to it for over an hour, pointing out life that I had never noticed. In that time, I came to realize that what I thought was nothing but waste water draining into the distant sewers, was actually teeming with life. Small fish that I never knew existed darted around, pursuing bugs I had never seen before. Salamanders would budge, totally surprising me. From that day forward I learned to pay closer attention to Mother Nature. She always surprises me with her richness and abundance. But Zak found himself floundering in a world previously hidden from him. Without close examination he pointed to a small pin cherry shrub, asking, "Is that the plant with the plant spirit?"

"You're guessing. I can see at least three others on the periphery. No, that's not it."

"I give up."

I knew it was time to leave, so I relented from pushing him any further. "It's right next to me," I said with my arms folded. With exaggerated movement I peered over my right shoulder at a small huckleberry-like bush that grew singularly alone, sporting a beauty not to be found anywhere else in the surrounding area.

"I used to bring people here when I conducted my classes, swearing them not to tell anyone about this spot. But in two years' time so many people had come to this location that they wore a noticeable path right where I'm standing. This track didn't used to be here. Because people were not careful and respectful of the gateway, it shut down. For three years. Only recently has it opened up again. So when I tell you not to let anyone know what you've seen today, I mean it. There are those who are called 'Gatekeepers' whose job it is to steward and protect such areas as this. The Gatekeeper who was the overseer and protector of this glen fell down on the job. I no longer have classes here. You are one of the very few I have shown the gateway and the Council Tree to since then. Please respect that. This is not public information. At least until people remember how to show reverence for the sacredness of Mother Nature."

"Thank you," Zak said with genuine humility. "How do you know all this stuff?"

"That's a story for another day. I believe it's time for you to head back to Denver. Am I right?"

Upon looking at his cell phone clock, he began texting a message to his next appointment. As he drove me back to the house, I decided to impress upon him one more point. This entailed a story I almost never told. The reason for keeping the story quiet stemmed from the inability of most people to trust that it even happened. And I can't blame them. At the time, even I was stretched to the limit of my belief systems. However, witnessing the powers of nature in ways that most don't know exist had eliminated any doubt I had about the extraordinary tales I had heard from Malidoma—tales of his initiation into his manhood and into the tribe while living in Burkina Faso. Though what I had to say wasn't important for Zak to believe, it was important for him to hear the message behind the story, so that he might broaden his awareness regarding his chosen career that involved the land. I felt it important for him to understand that the land was more than buying and selling. There came a deep responsibility to the land, especially when the land was involved with one's life purpose.

"I have one more story I'd like to tell you. Even though I know you will find it hard to believe, I want you to know every word is true." A smile crept across Zak's face.

THE STORY OF THE LAND AND LIFE

Years ago, a young man came to study with me—the first of the Quantum Kids I became aware of. He lived with me for nine months. It was the most bizarre nine months of my entire life. And I've had a bizarre life. Holding a black belt in kung fu, he knew discipline, yet he also had hidden himself in a life filled with drunkenness, drugs, and recklessness. Why he came to study with me stemmed from an encounter I had with him at a conference I had keynoted. He had volunteered in a display of quantum entanglement that I performed in front of the audience. It so shocked him that he kept pestering me for more information until the conference closed two days later, and I returned to Denver.

Upon returning home to Kansas, this nineteen-year-old, whom I will call Jesse, immediately drove to his best friend's apartment to tell him of his experience. Upon describing to his friend all that had happened, he noted the hour was late and, since his friend had to work the next day, decided to head for home. However, upon leaving the friend's apartment, a flash of light exploded out of nowhere, surrounding Jesse in unfathomable energy that overloaded his body. Before he hit the ground, he pounded on his friend's now-closed door. Upon finding the youngster on the ground, the friend dragged him back into the apartment and told him he was calling 911. The lad kept mumbling, "No, no, no." After about half an hour, he recovered, told his friend about the light, and once again decided to drive back to his parents' house.

As he got into his car, he noticed hundreds of crows flying around the lampposts above him. He knew crows don't fly at night, so this struck him as highly unusual. As he left the parking lot, the crows followed—and, further freaking him out, continued to follow for five more miles until he got home. Matters got even more frightening for him. This entire episode disturbed him so greatly that he ended up calling me at four in the morning. That phone call resulted in his quitting community college, leaving his job, and moving out to Colorado to study with me.

Jesse turned into an unbelievable protégé, learning the Way of One beyond his years. His serious studying of kung fu had prepared him for noticing unseen forces, and within ninety days he began assisting me with clients. The critical point in his growth occurred when he began picking up his own clients. At that point, I knew that the student had become the master, though it seemed to me that there was such a thing as progressing too quickly.

Because of the work I had done with a famous musician in the LA area, another call came from an equally unlikely source—two PhD psychologists—well, one, actually. The father didn't want to have anything to do with the phone call. The mother was desperate with worry. Her fifteen-year-old son was close to dying. He had acquired some kind of disease or condition in which he could not keep food or drink down, nor could he sleep more than minutes at a time. His entire body was covered in sores that itched unmercifully. If his condition didn't stop, he would soon die. The doctors could do nothing for him. No matter what they tried, he continued to get worse. Would Jesse and I fly down?

Two days later we arrived in LA. After checking into the hotel provided by the mother, we followed her directions to the house. She apologized right off for the absence of her husband, who refused to stay in the house as long as this charade of a voodoo farce continued under his roof. He would stay at a hotel, content to remain there until Jesse and I left.

When we checked out the son, lying limp on his bed, Jesse immediately leaned over to me and said, "Something is feeding on him." When I asked what, he shrugged his shoulders. The boy's story was heartbreaking to hear. He had suffered terribly, reminding me of my own ordeal with an incurable skin disease. It had been four days since he last was able to keep food down, and even then it went right through him. I decided the first thing he needed was hope, so I told him my own story and the appearance of the angel. He wanted to know right away if an angel was going to appear. Jesse stepped in and mumbled that he felt something else was in the room. That brought out the dowsing rods. Mother and son had never seen dowsing rods work before, thus bombarding us with several questions. Jesse grew impatient. The dowsing rods told me Jesse was correct. There was a consciousness in the room, unlike any I had detected before. After wrestling with several concepts to determine what the rods had picked up, the only words that would cause the rods to swing inward were "other-dimensional beings." The only reason I came up with such words stemmed from my work with my shamanic teacher, Malidoma Somé. In that moment, I realized I was in new territory, and from stories that Malidoma had told, the boy might not be the only one in danger.

After finalizing our introductions, Jesse wanted to go outside and check out the land. Within a minute he was pointing to the backside of the property. "It's there," he said.

"What?" I asked, not really noticing anything.

"The wormhole."

Such phenomena are rare. I've only discovered some nine of them in my twenty years of work. Even then, wormholes come in different forms—physical wormholes being the most rare. The Hopi and the Dagara both have legends that tell of the physical wormholes, which have been secretly guarded over centuries. Only the highly initiated of the tribe are ever told about them. As one legend has it, the Hopi wormhole connects Hopiland to the Southern California area, enabling a traveler to walk only a couple of hours to reach the Los Angeles Basin. Malidoma tells of a similar story.

Wormholes oriented around time or space are more ethereal, providing connections to alternate realties but not allowing physical travel. The dowsing rods told me the wormhole that Jesse was seeing was a space-time wormhole, the only such kind I have ever witnessed. And because of that, I had no idea what we were getting ourselves in for.

"It's going into the kid's room," Jesse pointed to the upstairs level.

"The wormhole?" My years of wisdom and the tales told to me by Malidoma were making me more and more cautious.

"Yes. It's coming out of his room and going over this high ridge." Jesse immediately began climbing a cliff behind the house. I decided to watch. When he got to the top of the escarpment, he stared toward the west and then at me. "It goes quite a ways. I think we should follow it. We need to find out where it's coming from. It's how the beings get into the kid's room. Will you come up here and see what you get?"

I was in no hurry to go climbing cliffs or to go after phenomena I was not familiar with. After climbing a fence, I found a way to the ridge that didn't involve mountain climbing. Uneasily, I sidled up to Jesse. It was then that I could feel the vibration coming off the wormhole, and it wasn't good. After checking my dowsing rods, I let Jesse know he was correct as to the direction of the wormhole. I also let him know that the dowsing rods indicated our following the wormhole was not in our best interest but was in the best interest of the boy.

"Ehhh. I'm not afraid. You taught me that much." And off he went.

Clumsily I followed him down one hill and up another, the ground parched from months of no rain. With every footfall, I began to hear swishing sounds. When I stopped, the brushing sound stopped. When I continued walking, the sound of something moving through the dead grass picked up again. "Do you hear that?" I yelled at Jesse, hoping he would stop and rest a moment. He was bent on finding where the wormhole started.

"Hear what?" he said, finally paying attention to me.

"That sound like something in the grass, following us."

"Oh, that. You haven't seen them?"

Normally, I am proud of any of my students when they begin to see the unseeable, the worlds beyond normal vision. But Jesse had far surpassed me. I found myself growing more annoyed with each discovery that he had failed to inform me of.

"Seen what?" I yelled, my voice going up an octave.

"Lizards. They're everywhere. Dozens and dozens following us."

"What? Are you kidding?" I immediately squatted down to look into the grass. Sure enough. Everywhere around me posed the little buggers, three to five inches long—leopard lizards, I would find out later. Within a five foot radius I counted at least ten. "Don't you think it a bit unusual that they're following us? Don't they usually scurry away?"

"Hell if I know," Jesse mused, then turned on his heel to continue his trek. I decided to check my dowsing rods. They told me to go no further. Finding a nearby rock, I decided to observe Jesse with the binoculars our host had provided. The hair on my arms stood at attention, and I felt no motivation to take another step.

The shuffling in the grass followed Jesse as he hoofed another 150 yards. Frankly, it creeped me out to hear the dozens and dozens of little lizards escorting him as if he were entering some kind of assembly hall. Worse, I noticed five vultures circling overhead. As I focused on their presence, they broke their circle and headed west. In the language of the Wyrd, this was a warning that the forces of death lingered nearby.

What I would discover after returning to Colorado was that the area we had found actually was a kind of place of sacred assembly. Like the Environmental Learning Center, the area we had discovered was known as the Seven Holy Hills by the Native tribes of the area. Like the sacred site on the ELC, the place Jesse had entered had also been known as a potlatch or chautauqua or powwow, a sacred place of peace where battles were forbidden. However, the energy I was feeling was anything but peaceful.

"It's here," Jesse yelled across the dale. "The wormhole starts here."

Immediately I put my dowsing rods to work. What I picked up surprised even me. I detected two gateways. Normally it takes a gateway or portal of some kind to feed a wormhole. But I had never seen two gateways next to one another. As I augured for more information, I realized that the second gateway was unnatural, artificial, located next to the natural gateway. I also detected that the unnatural gateway swirled with a heavy negative force and was about thirty feet to Jesse's left. I bellowed my information down to him, having to repeat a few sentences because of the distance.

"I'm going to check out the negative gateway," he hollered.

"I don't think that's a good idea," I yelled back. But to no avail. The man was fearless. As he stepped into the center of the swirling negative force, his feet began to stumble, and within a matter of a minute he fell to the ground. Alarmed, I stood immediately, sending a flank of lizards scurrying away. Through the binoculars, I could see his struggle to get up, sweat pouring off him. He looked my way, his eyes begging me to do something.

"Help me," he cried out. "I can't get up."

My mind went crazy. If he couldn't stand, how in the hell did he expect me to rescue him? Jesse was now a fit twenty-year-old who had demonstrated his strength more than once during our hikes to the sacred gateway above Boulder. He could lift me up as if I were a sack of wheat. I, on the other hand, was showing my years. It was all I could do to keep up with him on the high Rocky Mountain trails of the Flatirons, not far from where we lived. There was no way I was going to enter this negative gateway, this place of dimensional darkness. I had problems standing in a negative vortex. There was no way I could handle a negative gateway. But how was I going to help him?

"Jesse, my rods are telling me to stay out of there. See if you can crawl. If you crawl far enough, I'll come get you." He didn't move. I wasn't sure he heard my voice clearly across the distance. I began to pace back and forth. I couldn't use a cell phone. There was no reception. If I ran back to the house, it would be at least an hour before I got back to him. I couldn't take that risk. Perhaps I could run into the dark gateway, grab him as fast as I could, and drag him as far as I could in hopes he could recover enough to get the both of us out of there.

Just as I was about to bound down the slope to my struggling friend, Jesse started to move. Slowly he began to crawl on his hands and knees, then collapse, then crawl again. After about thirty feet of erratic efforts, I checked the dowsing rods. I could go after him. Like a bull elephant I charged down the hill to where he lay on the ground. The effects of the swirling forces started hitting me, weakening me. Without hesitation I grabbed one of Jesse's arms and began dragging him. After fifty feet, I had to stop to catch my breath. Jesse's heavy breathing began to ease. With shaking hands, I opened a new bottle of water and urged him to drink.

"That's better," he gasped. "Give me a few. I think I'll be able to walk." Five minutes later we both sat on my roost that had served as my observation post.

"Now what do we do?" I asked, realizing we had stumbled onto something neither of us had dealt with before. Frankly, I was disturbed that we were over our heads with an unknown danger. Self-preservation nagged at me to get the hell out of there. Leave. And leave now. But not Jesse.

"It has to be shut down," he said coldly. "It's helping to kill the kid. I saw the beings using the wormhole. They're like futuristic warriors from another dimension, covered in scales. They shouldn't be here. They are using the life force of the kid to further their own purposes. He's exceptional and doesn't know it. I don't think he's the first they've attacked, nor do I think he will be the last. This has to be stopped."

In all my years of working with alternate reality, I have witnessed the impossible over and over again. But this incident took the cake, the frosting, and the candles. Normally, when Quantum Kids tell me of the worlds they see, I treat their visions as metaphors. That allows me to avoid deciding whether to believe them or not. I simply interact with their metaphor as if it's an archetypal story or a poetic reality. I take what they tell me as if they are symbols, and then I translate the symbols into ordinary reality. That has served both them and me over the years quite well. But what Jesse was telling me struck me as beyond metaphor. He had been attacked, and I had felt the forces behind the attack. Our bodies were registering distinct threat, not negative archetypal metaphors, not poetic symbolism.

Then I remembered something Malidoma has said to me: "There is nothing greater than the fullness of Nature." At the time, I took his meaning to be poetic symbolism, even though he insisted it was far more than that. What if he were right? What if there were some way I could engage the Great Spirit of Nature to intercede for us?

"I think the only way to shut it down is to use the land," I said, not knowing at all what that might entail.

Jesse nodded his head. "You said you brought a set of stones for an angelic gateway. Do you happen to have them with you?"

"Actually, I do. They're in my fanny pack. I brought two gateways, just in case we might need to also construct a Gate of Light." I pulled out the stones and handed them to him.

"Help me put one together on top of the natural gateway," he said. "It's about forty or fifty feet away from the negative gateway. It's flat on the land, so we shouldn't have a problem constructing the angelic gateway on top of it. The negative gateway is stealing energy off the vortexes of the natural gateway to feed the wormhole." How he knew this, I could only guess. He'd already grown in his abilities to the point where I trusted him without putting him through interrogations.

So disorienting was the area around the natural gateway, that it took us another hour to lay out the stones for the angelic gateway. We finished as the sun began to set. As soon as the angelic gateway opened, the negative gateway shut down. Completely. Jesse looked at me with that devilish grin of his that showed his braces from end to end. "Not bad," was all he said as he began to gather up our belongings to head back to the house.

The mother came running to us hysterically as we climbed over her fence. "What happened to you two? You've been gone for five hours. I was just about to call Search and Rescue. Are you OK?"

Jesse looked like someone had dragged him through a barn. We explained our story as best we could without alarming the mother. After eating a sumptuous dinner she prepared, Jesse let her know that he thought her son would survive. He told her we had two more things to do before leaving. Then we would be back the next morning.

The mother watched as we constructed a Gate of Light above the headboard of her son's bed. I tried to explain to her how it worked. After all, she was a scientist of modern psychology who had dared to invite in a world beyond textbooks. Afterward, Jesse told the teenager to lie still and just allow grace to come into him. After explaining that grace is the essence of Diving Love, Jesse began moving his hands up and down along the boy's meridians. Jesse's hands began to shake violently as he entered a trance state. This state that he could enter was not something I understood or learned. He had recently discovered it on his own. I watched, holding space for him with my intent as he worked for twenty minutes in his altered state.

As we left for the night, Jesse instructed the mother to put a glass of water alongside a hard-boiled egg next to her son's bed. If he ate, great. If he didn't, then Jesse would do further work on the boy.

We both sat with silent exhaustion as we drove back to our hotel.

When we arrived the next morning, the mother wept as she opened the door. My first thought was that of dread. Had the boy died?

"I don't know what to say," she started. "He slept through the whole night for the first time in three months. He's eating breakfast. This is wonderful. Thank you both. Have you eaten?"

The conversation with the son was a celebration. The sores on his skin had already started sloughing off, his eyes no longer swollen from irritation. As skinny as he was, he looked so much better. In my listening to the fifteen-year-old, I heard cues telling me I should explore further. What I discovered was that the son had issues with his father. By using holodynes, the whole truth came out. The son loved his father greatly. But the father's dogmatism had totally shut down his son's ability to know himself, be himself, find himself. In spite of his love for his dad, the son feared his father and could say or do nothing about it. I encouraged the lad to trust in himself and his love for his father. The truth would serve him far better than silence or fear. Experience has taught me that the Quantum Generation admires wisdom above all else. If you speak to them directly and honestly, showing them wisdom as the light to quench any darkness around them, they will listen. And that's what happened.

The mother asked to be taken to the angelic gateway. She wanted to see what it looked like and she wanted to see the place where the wormhole had originated. I told her that the distance was great on foot, and asked her if there was a map of the hills we could look at to see if we could approach from a road nearby. After finding the nearest route, we headed out to the location that had previously taken down Jesse. As we climbed over a concrete culvert, I noticed a lizard sunning itself. However, it was the only lizard I saw. Unlike before, field birds now flew everywhere, a symphony of chirping contrasting greatly with the deadly silence and the lizards slithering through the grass the previous day. Not a vulture was to be seen. As we showed Mom the stones of the gateway, she remarked how wonderful the area felt, wondering how the same place could have been so threatening the previous day. Having witnessed the twilight zone of the previous day, I was indeed struck by the change. It was so remarkable that even I had a hard time believing in what had deeply shaken us less than twenty-four hours earlier. After giving the mother a diagram of where each stone sat in the sacred geometry, we headed back.

After Jesse did one more session with the shaking hands and left instructions that the Gate of Light was not to be taken down by the father, we both left. What we heard upon our return to Colorado was that the father had returned home the next day to find his son without scabs, walking around with growing strength, and able to sit down for dinner with the family. A confrontation developed over how such a change could have been possible, the father wanting to know the "full" truth—his version of truth. The son came right out and told his father that he had been afraid of him most of his life, and that he didn't want to be afraid of him ever again. He loved him, and he wanted their lives to be based on love from that day forward. The son asked his father to respect his ways and his ideas, his needs, his world. Much to the father's credit, he heard his son, and the boy thrived.

"The moral of these stories," I said to Zak as we coasted to a stop in front of the house, "is that the Way of One rises up out of the land. The Earth is more than our Mother or our Father. The earth is also our Teacher, our gateway to the fullness of life. We are meant to have life to the full. If you will learn this, then your world of business will grow in ways you never dreamt possible. And not only your world of business, but your personal world as well. If you will learn the Way of One, you will find the path to all things that will serve you to the full. Like King Arthur, you and the land are One."

KNOWING THE UNKNOWN

Some believe that the greatest of unknowns lies in outer space. Others believe the greatest unknowns lie in the depths of our oceans.

Yet others believe the atom itself holds the mystery of mysteries. The real point here is the word "believe." In work done by quantum physicist David Bohm, he proposes a notion called "holonomy" or the Law of the Whole. The premise behind holonomy is that the Fabric of the Universe is in a constant state of recreating itself, enfolding and unfolding upon itself in a never-ending regenerative motion. The implications of this "holomovement," this interconnected totality of all there is—what Bohm labels as "the ground of all that is"—confront the very notion of belief, and especially belief-oriented systems. When consciousness resides in this enfolding-unfolding wholeness, Bohm states there is no knowing, which connotes there can be no unknown (unknowing). Which means there can be no beliefs except those that support illusions, or what Hinduism calls "Maya."

PhD clients have always been the most difficult for me to work with. Not because they challenge my world of the unfathomable or the techniques I employ that go against the rational, but because they cannot get out of their own way—a way anchored in belief systems cloaked in the garment called "the scientific principle." What most PhDs don't know is that there is more than one scientific principle. And what they do not like to admit is that science has always been in a state of flux, unfolding to new discoveries or contraindications of their scientific world. I laugh at hearing the latest discovery that neutrinos can travel faster than the speed of light. At one fell swoop, the long-held scientific beliefs in Einsteinian physics becomes obsolete. This is the fate of all belief systems, and Bohm, as well as Bruce Lipton, tells us the sooner we let go of this archaic notion of systems based on belief, the better off we will be as individuals who make up the Law of the Whole.

How was Jesse able to see the unseeable? How did the fifteen-year-old son of two PhD psychologists crash the bastions of modern medicine and modern psychology? How was I able to use the land as a gateway into "the ground of all that is"?

There is a story I like to tell that I heard from fellow author Gregg Braden while attending the Prophets Conference in Port Townsend, Washington. There are variations of this story floating around, but I am particularly fond of my version of the story as I remember it.

Braden had received permission to witness a shamanic rainmaking ceremony, a privilege rarely given to anyone, let alone white folk. Arrangements were made to meet the shaman on top of a mesa during a time of severe drought in the Four Corners region of the Southwest. When Braden arrived the shaman instructed him to sit quietly on the ground while he began the ceremony. Closely watching the shaman's every move, Braden fixed on the shaman as he began honoring the four directions. But then the rainmaker just stood there, and stood there, and stood there, with eyes closed and breath measured.

Finally he opened his eyes and said to Braden, "We can leave. It is going to rain."

Braden wondered what had happened, if anything. "What did you do so that it will rain?"

The rainmaker's answer was, "I don't know."

After agreeing to meet the wrinkled gentleman the next morning for breakfast at the trading post—supposedly after the coming of the rain that night—Braden went back to his motel. Immediately he turned on the TV to get the weather report. The weatherman reported clear skies with no indication of relief from the drought in the foreseeable future. Disappointed, Braden turned off the TV and readied himself for bed. As he was about to fall asleep, he decided he would call the rainmaker in the morning and cancel breakfast. He had much to get caught up on back in Colorado.

Just before dawn, a horrible racket awakened Braden. It sounded like firecrackers going off on the corrugated tin roof. He jumped from his bed and dashed out the door to see if some perpetrator was playing a practical joke. Who would be setting off firecrackers at this hour in the morning? As soon as his feet hit the dirt, he realized that hailstones littered the ground. The sound on the roof was from hail bombarding the tin. Lightning erupted all around him. He jumped back inside just in time to avoid the downpour.

As he washed his feet and dressed, the only thought in his head was how the rainmaker had pulled off the impossible. Braden had to find out, and breakfast was yet a few hours away.

As the waitress took the order, Braden knew he could not press the Elder for information. It was against courtesy and protocol. He had sat in enough ceremonies with Native Elders to know that one operates on their time, not White People's time. The rainmaker had the grin of the cat that ate the canary as he enjoyed his coffee and bear claw pastry. Finally, he brought up the topic of the weather.

With carefully constructed dialog, Braden teased out of the rainmaker how the rains had fallen, even though the old guy had made it apparent the previous day that he did not know what he did that made the rains fall.

The rainmaker told Braden what transpired during the time of standing still while Braden had watched him the previous day. "I don't pray for rain," the rainmaker started out. "I pray rain. I open myself to the Great Spirit that rain may come through me. I have to be the rain. After singing to the four directions, I stand and wait. While waiting, if I can begin to feel raindrops on my skin then I wait until I can smell the wetness of the earth. If I can smell the wetness of the earth, then I wait until I can see the seeds of maize in the fields drinking from the wetness. If I can see the seeds of maize drinking from the moist land, then I wait until I can see the young shoots reaching for Father Sky. If I can see the shoots reaching for Father Sky, then I wait until I can hear the wind blowing through the stalks of corn. If I can hear the wind blowing through the stalks of corn, then I wait until I can smell the pollen from the tassels of fully grown plants. If I can smell the pollen, then I wait until I feel the green leaves and ripened maize brushing against me as I walk through the richness of the field full of blessing for my people. If I can feel the maize brushing against my face and stroking my chest while I walk through the field, then I know it is going to rain."

What struck Braden most profoundly was how the story had begun with the words "I don't know" but ended with the words "I know." Upon reflection, he realized that what the rainmaker had done was tap into Bohm's unfolding-enfolding universe by being able to know without knowing. Braden spent weeks contemplating the impact of what to-know-without-knowing had upon what we call reality. At the core of this phenomenon is the ability to trust. To trust with such trust that consciousness itself alters reality. Not what we believe reality to be, but what can pour forth from the abundant potential of all beingness.

Though quantum mechanics has no issue with this model, the scientific principle does. As a statistician I know that at the core of the scientific principle is what is called a hypothesis. The object of the research is to test whether the hypothesis is statistically significant, which means it meets the premise of the hypothesis, which is an expectation. The mere fact of establishing an expectation and establishing a way of measuring it—the hypothesis—already interferes with the potential (future) outcome (the Heisenberg Uncertainty Principle). In other words, the very premise of the scientific principle is faulty at its core because the expectation of the research alters the outcome of the research. Does that mean we quit doing scientific research? No. But it does mean that we keep it in perspective. We cannot and must not rule out the role of consciousness (the observer) in determining what is real.

As an example: In the 1940s it was thought humanly impossible to break the four-minute mile barrier. In 1954, twenty-five-year-old Oxford medical student Roger Bannister proved the world wrong. His demonstrating that the accepted limit was false caused a number of athletes to repeat his feat during the 1950s. Had human evolution all of a sudden changed magically during the 1950s? No. Perception had changed. Consciousness now dictated that the unthinkable was not only thinkable, but reachable. Today, even high-school athletes break the four-minute mile barrier. Since 1954 the fastest times in the mile have dropped some seventeen seconds. Sport in general is a testimonial that records (limits) are illusions even in the limited realm of the physical.

In the case of the two PhD parents, were their limits (cloaked in the name of science) serving them and their fifteen-year-old son? Or were the unexplainable "realities" brought in by Jesse serving their son? The bottom line in working with the ability to-know-without-knowing rests on the capability of trusting in the complete fullness of life wrapped in the holonomy of the Fabric of the Universe. What awaited me, I would find out years later, was a mind-blowing discovery of how each of us can open the door to this holonomy, this Law of the Whole. But a framework must be put in place before I can attempt to describe this.

Chapter 8

POWER BEYOND POWER

In 1999, the angels asked me to create a special oil that only I was to make, which was to be given to humankind. They said that the oil "is of the Christ, of Christ Consciousness." Thus I gave the oil a name—the "Christ Oil." Because my abilities to communicate with the angels were not what they are now, they gave the instructions for making this sacred oil to Joseph Crane, who in turn passed the instructions on to me. Other oils were introduced by the angels, also to be made exclusively by other individuals. But of all the oils that came from the angelic realm from 1998 to 2002, the Christ Oil was the only one that was not ritually applied with fingers. Instead the palms of the hands were to be used.

The making of this oil required three days. It involved the mixing of four pure oils and a sacred blessing that I was to recite over the blend. The mixture, which could only be made on a Friday, was to be put in a sacred place of my choosing after sunset. The oil was not to be touched at all on Saturday, the day during which the angels would add their blessing to it, but could be retrieved from the sacred place on Sunday after sunrise. After retrieving the bottle, I could always tell when the angels had visited, for the Christ Oil always contained within it a small white bone-looking object in the shape of a wing that wasn't there before.

To those who wished to anoint themselves with this oil, a specific ritual was to be used. A drop was to be placed on the palm of each hand, with one hand then placed over the heart and the other over the brow or third eye. These words were then to be spoken: "As a Child of God, I open my mind and my heart to the Christ Consciousness that I may live in the same light."

At the time, I did not realize the power behind the oil and the ritual that went with it. The palms of the hands, it turns out, have great meaning across cultures as a gateway through which power flows. In the case of this angelic ritual, it is the power to unite both mind and heart, the bringing together of the great forces of duality. Traditionally, the left hand (receiving) represents the archetypal feminine, while the right hand (giving) represents the archetypal masculine. In bridging the duality that is within us, we are then able to bridge all duality surrounding us. The Christ is the symbol of Oneness: "There are many parts but one body." (1 Cor. 12:20)

In Joseph Campbell's book, *The Mythic Image* (Princeton University Press, 1981), he speaks specifically about the palm that holds the symbol of the eye:

Interpreted in Oriental terms, its central sign would be said to represent the "fear banishing gesture" of a Bodhisattva hand showing on its palm the compassionate Eye of Mercy, pierced by the sight of the sorrows of this world. The framing pair of rattlesnakes, like those of the Aztec Calendar Stone, would then symbolize the maya power binding us to this vortex of rebirths, and the opposed knots would stand for the two doors, east and west, of the ascent and descent, appearances and disappearances, of all things in the endless round. Furthermore, the fact that the eye is at the center of the composition would suggest, according to this reading, that compassion is the ultimate sustaining and moving power of the universe, transcending and overcoming its pain.

Like Campbell's hand of the Bodhisattva, each of us possesses within us the "compassionate Eye of Mercy." And likewise, each of us holds within us "the ultimate sustaining and moving power of the universe." But how many of us actually trust such a statement? Dare I say, few? If any? How can a single human hold the power of the universe? Maybe it's time to explore that.

THE STORY BEHIND CHERYL

The snows of Colorado can come at any time, even in summer months. In this case, the summer of 2008 had just exited a few weeks earlier with the weatherman forecasting up to a foot of snow over the October 3rd weekend. Cheryl had just hung up the phone and left a message with the gentleman who had paid to use her southwest pasture for his fifty head of black heifers. She had suggested in the message that he might wish to come pick up his cattle early, because of heavy snow approaching. Arrangements had already been made for him to pick up the herd the coming Tuesday. With the approaching weather, the heifers would need feed, and Cheryl wasn't sure she had enough if he couldn't make it in through the snowstorm. Already she had noticed the herd nudging the fences to access more grass. If it weren't for the fact that they were soon due for pickup, she'd consider moving them to another pasture just to avoid the expense of repairing fencing if their nudging went too far. It was not her responsibility to feed the herd. Her first priority was her horses in the other pastures.

As she stared at the phone, her thoughts turned toward feeding herself. Time to head into Fort Collins to stock up on food. The expanse of the Legend Trail Ranch snuggles against Highway 287, some twenty miles north of the nearest grocery store on the outskirts of the city. With a foot of snow coming, she needed to stock enough supplies in case of an emergency. Before leaving, she checked with her ranch manager, Sandy, to see if she needed anything.

Cheryl is one of my closest friends. Her husband's death a few years earlier had left her to manage the 1500-acre ranch alone. Her hiring

Sandy Lagno as ranch manager fulfilled two purposes: Sandy was willing to live in the ranch house (Cheryl could use the company on the large spread), and Sandy had a reputation as an expert horsewoman, having trained horses all her life, which would be a boon to Cheryl's horse raising business. Some would call Sandy a horse whisperer, though she would bristle at such a term. What she does with horses extends beyond talking to them. She can actually connect with them, knowing their thoughts, as well as letting them know hers. As the author of *Horses: From Our Side of the Fence* (Beneficence, Inc., 2007), she reveals the language of horses. However, let it be known that I've seen her communicate with dogs, cats, and cattle as well. Though it's tempting to dismiss such abilities, the evidence speaks for itself. Sandy is gifted.

As Cheryl drove her SUV along the mile-long dirt road across her property, she automatically scanned the pastureland making sure the solar-powered pump had filled the water tanks and that the mineral feeder had enough supplements for the herd. The pastoral scene comforted her as she turned onto the highway to head into town. The highway skirted along the southwestern part of her land, and as she accelerated her vehicle to get up the hill, she noticed there was no sign of the cattle— anywhere. *Maybe they broke through one of the fences*, she considered. She would check again on her return.

Darkness had begun to descend and the snow had already started to coat the ground as she rumbled back onto the dirt road. She had slowed down on the highway to check for the black heifers in the south leg of the ranch. Still nothing. The dirt road traversed a ridge that led to the large ranch house. From this vantage, Cheryl could see the remaining 500 acres of the south pasture where the cattle roamed. Not a heifer anywhere.

Maybe Sandy had seen them. Removing the glove from her right hand she pulled the cell phone from her purse and called Sandy.

"Hi. Have you seen any of the heifers today? I can't seem to find them."

"Now that you mention it, I haven't seen hide nor hair of them all day. I haven't ridden the southern leg, however. Maybe they're trying to shelter against the ridge over there."

"Nope," Cheryl answered. "I checked that out from the highway. They aren't there either. Have you noticed any fence-breaks at all?"

"No. I've checked all the horses in the other pastures and have given them hay. Haven't seen any problems anywhere."

Really strange, Cheryl thought as she hung up.

As best she could, she peered at the length of fences to spy a break anywhere in the fencing. Everything looked intact. While parking the SUV in the south garage, she realized the storm was starting to rage. There was no way she could saddle up one of the horses to do a quick check of the other pastures. She'd see what the morning would bring.

Architecturally, Cheryl's ranch house is a horseshoe-shaped wonder that she herself designed, working with the spirits of the land. It sits on one of the mesas with an immense view to the north, east, and west. Large picture windows provide a breathtaking panorama of nature at her best. Just below the north wing rests a small lake, the guest bedrooms overseeing the flocks of birds that often visit its waters. In the middle of the horseshoe fans a marvelous tiled plaza with a three-tiered fountain. I never grow tired of the view of thousands of untouched acres whenever I visit.

At morning light, Cheryl picked up the binoculars she always keeps next to the dining room window. From that vantage she could see the watering tanks as well as the mineral feeder. Eventually, the missing herd would have to return for nourishment. But nothing—all day long. More than a foot of snow covered the surrounding valley with drifts several feet deep in some places. The previous warmth of the ground had created sheets of ice underneath the snow. For her and Sandy to ride horses would be too dangerous to attempt. Even using the four-wheel-drive truck was out of the question. Cheryl began to worry. Two days had passed without a heifer in sight, having no access to food.

Unbeknownst to Cheryl, Sandy decided to use a technique that two friends had used numerous times with clients who had lost animals. Like the creation of elementals or the calling forth of a holodyne, the technique involves combining intent with consciousness. They ask the client to focus on a place where the animal could return to—a place where it would be found. The owner had to refrain from worrying about what troubles or trauma might have befallen their animal, for that would cause the consciousness to create "form" around worrying, instead of providing a way home. This form of conscious intent sets up a kind of quantum beacon whereby the consciousness of the lost animal becomes connected (entangled) with the place of being found. Repeatedly throughout the weekend, Sandy would quietly focus her intent on the mineral feeder as a location where the herd could be found.

Sunday morning brought with it brilliant sunlight, raising temperatures. But no herd. Cheryl's mind searched for some explanation other than their breaking through a fence and wandering into an adjoining pasture. Someone would have contacted them by now if that were the case. Much of the ranch abuts the growing presence of Nature Conservancy plots. The valley sustains a diminishing environment where water and grasslands support Colorado native species. The Nature Conservancy does not look kindly upon cattle interfering with natural habitat. A growing uneasiness between ranchers and the Conservancy heightens with every new acquisition by the environmental organization. So, neither ranchers nor the Conservancy has a problem letting the other know if irregularities show up on each other's lands.

As Cheryl set the binoculars down for the umpteenth time, she realized that some kind of action needed to be put in place. Fifty head of cattle disappearing was no small matter. Cheryl decided to call her brother-in-law, Dave, to see if he would truck over to her place with a horse and go looking for the missing heifers. He could handle the weather-ridden terrain better than she or Sandy. After questioning Cheryl for possible reasons why black cattle couldn't be spotted on white snow, he agreed to arrive the next morning.

Hoping the herd might still be seeking out water, Cheryl spent the rest of Sunday scoping out all areas of the land from her vantage on the mesa. Sandy and Cheryl both have an incredible love for animals, and that love goes beyond duty or business. Any animal on their property, whether wild or domesticated, always received their affection, respect, and attention.

A couple years before, Cheryl had made the front page of the Fort Collins *Coloradoan* for her work in keeping horses alive during the West Nile virus epidemic. When others in the state were losing their horses to the disease, she developed a regimen to keep them alive and healthy.

Even when a vaccine became available later, she stuck to her techniques of working with the horses themselves using what is known in the medical community as kinesiology. The horses preferred her natural treatments. Cheryl's unique abilities of using natural means to heal animals provided her a high degree of respect with local veterinarians, who would often call her or work with her. And time after time she would leave the "docs" scratching their heads about her successful results.

Bright and early Monday morning, Cheryl got up to take care of chores. With the snow melting, she felt a sense of relief. She and Sandy would be able to search for the cattle, along with Dave, once Cheryl returned from a morning appointment she had in Fort Collins. So far, still no sign of the herd.

After showering and grabbing a bite to eat, Cheryl jumped into the SUV and slushed her way down the ranch road heading to the highway. As she turned a bend, giving her full view of the mineral feeder and water tanks, she spied the herd heading toward the mineral feeder in single file. Sliding to a halt, she started counting. *All present and accounted for*, she said to herself. Immediately she phoned Sandy to let her know that the heifers had found their way back and were heading to the mineral feeder. Cheryl couldn't see it, but Sandy had a knowing smile hearing where her friend had spotted the herd.

Excited, Sandy told Cheryl that she'd head down to the water tanks to check them out. Cheryl continued watching as long as she could. After visiting the mineral feeder, the heifers now made a beeline to the water tanks, again in single file. Grabbing her cell phone once again, Cheryl called Dave to let him know that all fifty head had returned. He decided he'd still drive to the ranch to check out the cattle and fences with Sandy. After all, the owner was due to pick up his herd the next day. No need to lose them again. Comforted, Cheryl continued on her way to town.

After finishing her appointment in Fort Collins, she rushed through her other affairs in town to get back to the ranch. Just before heading back on Highway 287 her phone rang. It was Dave.

"Listen. I've got some good news, and I've got some strange news."

"What's going on?" Cheryl grew anxious.

"Well, you'll be glad to know that there isn't a break in a fence anywhere. Which is kind of strange when you think about it. But it gets even stranger. When I decided to follow their tracks in the snow to where they had been hiding, I come to find out that there are no tracks. It's as if they magically appeared out of thin air about a couple of yards from the mineral feeder. Sandy is here with me. And she can't find a track in a hundred yards. Sonuvabitch, I don't know where they were or where they went. I gotta tell ya', this one's a head scratcher."

After hanging up her cell phone, Cheryl pondered the implications of what on God's green Earth was going on. She knew Dave's stockman skills and she knew Sandy's eye for detail. If the two of them said that an entire herd had appeared from out of the blue, then that's what had happened. She sped back to ranch, drove as close as she could to the water tanks, and headed to where the cattle were still gulping water. They acted as though they hadn't drunk in four days—which was the case. Like Dave and Sandy, she saw where the tracks started in the snow, as if out of nowhere. She checked and double-checked around the entire pasture to see if she could pick up any telltale signs in the pristine snowfall. None. That's when she decided she'd better give me a call.

I arrived at the ranch, dowsing rods in hand, four days after the cattle had reappeared. Indian summer had melted any hint of snow. As usual, Cheryl greeted me with a warm embrace as I met her at the ranch house.

"Well," she started, "you and I have been through some strange events in the past, but this one takes the cake. How can fifty head of heifers completely disappear for four days?" Cheryl has always been the kind of person who likes answers. Mystery may have its place, but if there is an answer to be had, she'll seek it out.

As a geomancer, I first try to pick up any anomalies that I feel in my body before I start using my dowsing rods. This technique more quickly attunes me to what may be behind the abnormality. Cheryl escorted me to the mineral feeder to pick up the scent, as it were. As I walked in concentric circles, nothing seemed out of the ordinary. After circling the third time, about twenty yards from the mineral feeder, I felt the familiar tingling in my body, most likely a geomagnetic anomaly. With concentration, I began to find the defining edges of what triggered the tingling. I discovered that the shape of the anomalous area formed a kind of long, narrow rectangle that pointed to the southwest. Pulling out my dowsing rods, I began asking questions about the source of the geomagnetic aberration. The rods told me that a wormhole had been here. Further questions revealed that it had been what I call a "type 3 wormhole," which means that both time and space had been altered, as opposed to just time (type 1) or just space (type 2). My reasoning told me that if I could find the source of the wormhole (in similar fashion as Jesse and I had found the source of the lizard wormhole), I could get more answers. This was the first time I had ever found the remnants of a type 3 wormhole.

American theoretical physicist, Michio Kaku, of whom I am a great fan, puts into understandable words how such things as wormholes can exist. In his book, *Physics of the Impossible: A Scientific Exploration into the World of Phasers, Force Fields, Teleportation, and Time Travel* (Anchor, 2009) he states the following on page 211:

> In 1988 Kip Thorne and colleagues at Cal Tech found an example of a transversable wormhole, that is, one through which you could pass freely back and forth. In fact, for one solution, the travel through a wormhole would be no worse than riding on an airplane.... In the last few years an astonishing number of exact solutions have been found to Einstein's equations that allow for wormholes.

A growing body of evidence from tests done in quantum physics labs points to phenomena previously relegated to science fiction. As a mathematician, I have a more-than-average respect for theoretical physics. As a man who has witnessed the impossible repeatedly, I find it high time to openly discuss with people a world beyond belief. With friends like Cheryl, I am able to do more than just discuss; I am able to share events heretofore kept secret.

A hike over the ridge took us to the southwest leg of the pasture, where I to looked for signs of where the cattle had been, even if that meant in another space-time continuum. It didn't take long for me to discover telltale signs of a natural gateway. What surprised me was that the gateway was not on the ground but on the face of a red cliff.

However, like gateways on the ground, all the bushes around the gateway pointed right to it. When I pointed it out to Cheryl, she thought I was saying that the cattle had caused the bushes to lean toward the cliff. Upon correcting her, I also pointed out how the remaining grass lay matted down by the snow.

"Notice that the grass isn't flat in only one direction. Notice how it makes a swirl?"

Cheryl was well-versed on gateways. Not only had she attended my classes at the Environmental Learning Center, years ago she had paid me to come out and check out the ranch land. Repeated strange incidences had caused her to wonder about the sacredness of the ranch, and why she felt so attached to it. It was as if she were governess over this magnificent display of Mother Nature's wonder. The first gateway I had discovered on the ranch lay over in the eastern portion on one of the knolls. What had led us to the spot was repeated circling over the area by white pelicans. People might wonder what pelicans are doing in Colorado. In truth, major flyways from Canada to Mexico cross Colorado as pelicans migrate from one region to another. These migration routes are determined by major ley lines that the flocks follow. The area around Legend Trail Ranch proved to harbor several ley lines, and with them associated geomagnetic phenomena. It's not unusual to see an entire flock of pelicans feeding and resting on the lake below the ranch house. But to see them spiraling in the sky over an area that has no food and no safety is reason to pay attention. And sure enough, the pelicans led us to the first gateway on the ranch. Cheryl felt the energy around this gateway to be gentle, comforting, and feminine. So she named the gateway the "Bird Woman Gateway."

The second gateway we discovered lay in the central part of the ranch. We found it in similar fashion as the first. This time, hawks and eagles repeatedly flew over an area that contained shale deposits. Shale can harbor crystalline structures within it. And where there's crystal, there is electromagnetic energy. Where there's electromagnetic energy, ley lines can be involved. Remember that it takes crossing ley lines and vortexes to create a gateway. Unlike the Bird Woman Gateway, this gateway contained active energy, almost unnerving, and strongly masculine. Cheryl dubbed this gateway the "Phoenix Gateway."

The third gateway, Cheryl found. That gateway was angelic in nature, meaning that the area served as a conjoining of heavenly and earthly vibrations or energies. This is not to be confused with the angelic gateway that the angels taught us how to make with sacred geometry. The gateway on the land was "natural" rather than constructed using precious stones or people. Cheryl called the three gateways the "Bird People Gateways," since winged beings of one form or another had led to their discoveries.

Note how in the last chapter how two gateways had been used to create the wormhole. In this case, four gateways had been used to create the wormhole. But by whom? In the case of the lizard wormhole, the beings behind its misuse were scalelike multidimensionals. What would we find in this case? Had harm come to the herd? Were they used in similar fashion as the fifteen-year-old kid? I let Cheryl know that we needed to tread carefully.

We decided to circle around to get to the top of the cliff. Once there, I began putting my dowsing rods to work, checking out every detail to make sure we were walking on hallowed ground rather than cursed ground. What I noticed was a large amount of dolomite limestone. Limestone, a sedimentary rock containing calcium/magnesium carbonate from millions of dead shellfish of the Paleozoic era, can also contain crystalline dolomite, a calcium magnesium carbonate that can also form with iron.

I picked up one of the larger stones and commented mistakenly to Cheryl, "This looks like a form of alabaster."

"That's possible. There are old alabaster mines east of the ranch. You can see the gravel quarry behind us. This land contains lots of rock formations."

"What my rods tell me," I commented, "is that there is a large crystalline vein beneath us. It's either alabaster or dolomite limestone." A week later, Cheryl checked to find that the stone was actually limestone.

"I'd like to show you something about the cliff." I then took her to the edge. "You see how red the rock and dirt are here? That means they're rich in iron. Given all the iron and limestone, I believe strong vortexes exist here because of ley lines and crystalline-based stone."

"How does that account for the disappearing herd?" Cheryl was trying to understand what I was implying when I, myself, wasn't sure.

My first order of business was to find out what beings were behind the use of the gateways and the wormhole. While planting myself over the crystalline vein, I began working my rods steadily, carefully acquiring the picture of what actually happened in this very active part of the land. Similar to the Environmental Learning Center, the land here held sacred purpose. Throughout the region, shamans constantly had sought vortical hot spots where sacred ceremony and high ritual could and would be used. Between the pelican gateway and the raptor gateway, we had found the remnants of an ancient medicine wheel, which told us that long before Whites claimed ownership of the land, Native peoples must have considered it sacred. And one could easily understand why. From my repeated visits, I had found the ranch to be a place of refuge, a place of peace. However, the spot of the lizard wormhole also had been sacred to Natives at one time. I still needed to determine who had used or misused the land to abscond with fifty head of cattle.

In my real estate work, I developed a pattern to rapidly get to the bottom of troublesome events in houses. I started with a list of categories:

- Is the imbalance or anomaly due to geomagnetic forces?
- Electromagnetic forces?
- Ancestors?
- Angels?
- Other-dimensionals?
- Feng shui?
- Karma?
- Construction problems?
- Or phenomena I am not familiar with?

When I started dowsing over the crystalline vein, running through the list in my mind, I expected that the rods would give me a yes on the last item on the list—something unfamiliar. In past situations in real estate, I've come across very few situations in which I found myself in unknown territory, but it happens. I expected this to be one of them.

However, the dowsing rods surprised me when they swung inward when asked if the source was angelic. *Well, at least I'm not dealing with another lizard wormhole,* I thought.

Once I determine a category on the list, there's yet another list to break down the information even further. In this case, I spent a good half hour determining the mystery behind the disappearing heifers. Explaining this to Cheryl would take some time.

As I looked up from the ground, Cheryl's eyes drove through mine. She could tell I had the answer, and she wanted to know what it was. Now.

"I think we should sit and talk for a while. How about we sit on a couple of boulders over by the cliff?" As we tried to find a comfortable position on the boulders, I began to knit together words that would explain what was going on.

Throughout my career as an author, I have written repeatedly about the angelic realm. What I have not done is speak of aspects of the angelic worlds that go beyond beliefs, that go beyond common knowledge, that go beyond myths and legends. Starting in 2006, a series of unexplainable events began in Colorado. Why Colorado? In *The Masters Return*, I write about a pronouncement by the angels that there will exist in the New Millennium seven Halls of Healing and Enlightenment. Colorado is one of those areas. In June of 2006, a gathering of like-minded people came together in Estes Park for what was called the Eden Event. The angels asked for nine of these events, starting in 2003. The last event occurred in 2011 in Arkansas. But what was so unique about the 2006 event was the return of the Shekinah to the earth. Having witnessed this return, and the results that came with it, I began to notice continuing occurrences of unexplainable phenomena centered around angelic beings. Each year after 2006 these phenomena would grow more powerful and more human-interactive. Words like "power of joy," "compassionate wisdom," and "love that passes understanding," began to be associated with these puzzling episodes where beings heretofore unseen began appearing to different groups.

One of the groups of beings I will discuss is called the "Seraphei Seraphim," or Seraphim of the Seraphim, not unlike the term "King of Kings." Normally, people have only heard of the seraphim, usually described as having four faces or four heads, along with six wings, accompanied by wheels of fire and hundreds of eyes on their wings. Legends have attached names to this little known group of the angelic realm, such as the Lords of Fire. In other writings they are called the Lords of Time or Time Lords. Still other translators of sacred texts call them the Dragons of Heaven or the Fiery Serpents. The point is that they exude great power and command great awe by anyone who has seen them.

Like the Shekinah, the Seraphei Seraphim have also returned to the earth. The reason for the return of these divine beings stems solely from humanity itself. As a student of prophecy since my teen years, I've kept track of every form of prophecy that has any credibility over the years. Whether you look at the information from ancient to modern-day prophets, to the technology revealed by whistleblowers from the National Security Agency (the Looking Glass Project) and other intelligence agencies (Project Pegasus, Project Lotus, or Project Yellow Book), all of them had foretold of the demise of our world in one form or another. That is, until the year 2008.

In 2008, a number of angelic appearances described how the angelic realm wished to work with humanity in fostering an era that would alter all aspects of prophecy before then. They spoke of the Ascension of the Earth and the co-creation of a New Eden. That year a global unity event called "The Gathering of One" worked in concert with the angelic realm to pilot in a shift of timelines. An entire book could be dedicated to the story of the shift of timelines, and how our world hung in the balance. But to keep a complex story as simple as I can, I'll just state that the Lords of Time, the Seraphei Seraphim, began showing up. From here on out, I will simply call them Seraphei.

Because of this unheralded teamwork between the angelic realm and certain groups of humans throughout our planet, we now rest in a new timeline that does not include the destruction of humanity or other Armageddon scenarios. Those will occur in a different quantum timeline separate from our world. Because of my many contacts with the Quantum Generation (often labeled "Indigos"), I knew early on that very tall beings with blue skin and immense power were showing up to certain people, proclaiming that a New Heaven and New Earth have come forth. Like the angelic realm, they did not get hung up on what they should be called. However, they are called "Seraphei Serphim" (or simply "Seraphei") by those who are best able to describe them using our language. These beings readily agreed that they were associated with the angelic realms (plural). And that others would come from yet other realms and would be appearing as Earth moved into its new destiny. One of the people that the Seraphei showed up to was Jake. His detailed description of them began to align with similar appearances to others. Not long after that, strange incidences began occurring at Legend Trail Ranch, and the beings associated with those incidences identified themselves as Seraphei to Cheryl.

As Cheryl and I sat looking over the cliff where the cattle had been shrouded, I stammered for an opening. "You know that you and I have talked before about these beings that have begun showing up. The Seraphei. That's who's behind the disappearance of the herd."

Cheryl looked at me like I had just stepped off a movie screen. "Why would angels have anything to do with a herd of heifers?"

"It's not about the heifers. It's about you. Tremendous forces are at play in our world right now. We have lived on a planet governed by fear, determined by wars, ruled by hatred. Those days are over. We may not see it just yet, but they are over. Whether you know it or not, whether you like it or not, this land that you have shepherded, the animals you have for so long cherished and cared for represent a metaphorical shift as to how humanity at large must learn to recognize Mother Earth.

"When you add to that the work you have put in to develop the Bless Your Heart line of products as a means and mechanism of spreading blessing wherever you go, to all you come in contact with, you have yet another metaphor as to how we must begin to see one another in this world—as blessings to one another—as vehicles for compassion and love, as instruments of blessing. What all of humanity ought to realize is that tremendous forces are here to assist all of humanity, as well as to be assisted by humanity. And I know that's a strange notion to folks. But truthfully, what I've seen over the last three years is that the angelic realm is telling us that they need us as much as we need them for this grand wonder to find completeness between Heaven and Earth. The heifers were nothing more than a sign to you and anyone who knows you that you are a powerful source for this message to come into flow."

Cheryl looked off into the distance as my words tapped on her heart. Emotions began to rise in her. She and I had dialogued before over fine wine and cheese, while kicking back and gazing from the back veranda at the wonder of the land on warm summer nights. We had spoken of how she shrank from her own power. As much as she knew that power coursed through her, she also knew that it terrified her. And now the two of us were revisiting this topic at a level beyond anything we had discussed before. No longer were we confronted with the notion of personal power. Now we found ourselves confronted with the notion that we were being visited by a power beyond power—of Divine Compassion—Love that passes understanding.

"I don't get it," Cheryl retorted. "I mean I get that the power of blessing, the power of love and compassion, are important, even transformational, but I don't get why fifty head of cattle? And why me?"

As I stared at the swirl of grass below us, I knew that this very statement from my dear friend reflected the entire consciousness of our world. "Why me?" Almost everyone thinks someone else is far more gifted, far more deserving, far more powerful to transform our world. And I use the word "transform" on purpose. Transformation comes out of trusting fully who we are, while change comes about through action. Trusting fully in oneself opens up the quantum potentials for having intent alter reality, as I've tried to strongly illustrate in preceding chapters. Moving into action may bring about change, but is it lasting, is it effective, and is it what's best for all involved? One of Cheryl's favorite sayings, stuck on her office wall, comes from tennis legend Billie Jean King: "Don't confuse movement with action." Similarly, Yoda instructs Luke Skywalker, "Do or do not. There is not try." Inasmuch as I would suggest to Yoda to alter his instruction to Luke to reflect the higher path—"Do not. Be." I would also say to Billie Jean King, "Don't confuse doing with being."

Oftentimes, when I find that clients are not fathoming a message coming from a holodyne (the self) or from a condition confronting them, I will switch away from having clients focus on themselves, and instead, turn myself into a version of their story that they might observe. That's what I decided to do with Cheryl.

"Cheryl, I'd like to tell you a story about myself that may get across what the Seraphei are trying to tell you. I've never told this story in public—only to a very few privately. Maybe it's time for me to reveal this hidden part of me as much as it may be time for you to do the same."

THE STORY OF THE POWER OF BECOMING (THE POWER TO BE)

Years ago, after Julia Ingram and I had written *The Messengers*, an incident occurred that later caused me to write the sequel of this international bestselling book that I titled, *The Days of Wonder* (DreamSpeaker Creations, 2003). In *The Messengers*, I talk about the return of the Apostle Paul in the personage of one Nick Bunick. But what I did not talk about was the return of other apostles whom I ran into while writing the book. Truthfully, it was tough enough trying to convincingly portray an amazing story to the general public that this hallmark figure from the time of Jesus (whom I prefer to call "Jeshua" rather than the Greek rendition—Jesus) had reincarnated. The subject of reincarnation is difficult to understand as it is. But to try and provide the same level of documentation used with Bunick to these other figures was beyond the book, and, frankly, beyond me.

One of the other figures from the time of Jeshua had persuaded Julia and me to convene with the reincarnated apostles Philip and Bartholomew at a seaside location on Bainbridge Island, a ferry ride's distance from Seattle. The purpose of the convocation was to have Julia pilot a group hypnotic-regression session so that we might see what new information might come forth from the collective effort. The idea had been enticing when first proposed to me, but then I remembered why I kept myself out of the original story. My purpose for co-authoring the book was not to draw attention to myself but to bring forth a message that supplemented Jeshua's original teachings by providing greater detail about them not found in other historical or religious documents. I went to great lengths to keep any information about my past from the public. Was it time to release that hidden information? Perhaps not, I thought.

Rather than cancel the meeting at Bainbridge, I decided to suggest that the others could engage in group hypnosis while I stayed an observer. Julia then intervened and stated that she wouldn't mind holding individual sessions, making sure there would be no biasing of the information, and if the information coming out of the sessions warranted it, she would play back all the tapes to the group afterwards. This I agreed to.

I was the third of four to enter Julia's session room. Before we began, Julia said a kind of prayer of intent, as she always did, that both she and I would be protected and guided by what would best serve me as we began the session. Once I entered an induced state, Julia asked if we might see pertinent information around the Master known as Jeshua. My mind saw the scene of men to my left wearing Biblical garb. To my right sitting on the floor next to me sat a woman with long, beautiful hair. The men were arguing. My feelings rose in me as I watched the scene, disturbed by the verbal jostling of the men. Julia began asking questions. Who were these men, and what could I tell her about the room? Who was the woman? The questions moved my mind more deeply into the event. Jeshua had died. The men were quarreling about who should be in charge. I could tell what they were thinking, one feeling he had a right to be in charge. Another felt he held the ability to carry forth the teachings better than the rest, and yet another felt that Jeshua had most favored him. They were struggling for power.

I told Julia that the woman next to me was the Magdalene, known as Miriam. Like me, she also felt distaste for what was transpiring. More than anyone in the large room, she understood real power, the kind of power addressed by Jeshua. I began describing the room for Julia in detail. Besides knowing what the apostles were thinking, I also could tell what Miriam was thinking as I rendered more and more specifics. This was the Upper Room, the place where the Last Supper had previously occurred.

While in conversation with Miriam, a strong feeling interrupted my discourse. I turned my head and stared across the room at a small ball of light starting to appear on the wall. As the ball grew in intensity so did the feeling of love. Now everyone could see the light starting to turn brilliant. The immensity of the love coming from the light began to overwhelm me. I had known this love before. It was Jeshua. The light began yielding as his form started to take shape. I snapped out of the hypnosis, gasping for breath.

Julia's eyes blinked big with concern. She asked me if everything was OK. I told her that Jeshua's love was more than I could handle as I started weeping. She tried to comfort me but what really stirred inside of me was beyond her understanding. My mind swam for comprehension of what I had just witnessed. It was as if some kind of giant cathedral door had been opened, never to be closed again. The magnificence of Jeshua's love could never be forgotten now that I once again knew its presence, its wonder, its complete and total imprint upon me. My body started shaking uncontrollably.

After Julia waited for me to calm down, she asked if she could begin the induction once again, take me back to the Upper Room. I told her she didn't need hypnosis to accomplish that. I could still vividly see the room, its inhabitants, and every bit of detail, including Jeshua now talking to everyone. After relating to her what I was seeing, she asked me how I knew what the other Apostles were seeing.

Carefully, I began to describe to her my ability, my gift that I carried. I called it the "Power of Becoming." As best as I could describe it, I told Julia how long ago I had discovered that I possessed the ability to enter into what I called the Oneness, even in my present life. Once I picked up the vibration of the person I was focusing on, I could start to feel their feelings, and sometimes even hear their thoughts. Deep inside of me, I knew I could never use this ability for my own personal gain. If I did, I would lose it. This "becoming" had to be centered in love, or the Oneness could not be achieved. Even though I had been disturbed under hypnosis at the behavior of the Apostles, I also felt a deep sense of compassion for their confusion, their worry, their sense of loss over Jeshua's death. I wanted to tell them that these negative traits prevented them from walking in Jeshua's shoes. They thought leadership was control when in truth Jeshua had shown the exact opposite. Leadership was about inspiring, not controlling.

Julia then asked me, "If you have this gift of becoming, does that mean you can become Jeshua?"

I looked at her stunned that she would even suggest such a possibility. Thoughts from 2,000 years ago mixed with my present thoughts. Should I even dare to answer her question? Great forces teetered within me, suggesting this was the time to reveal such an answer. After struggling with myself over the consequences of telling her, I finally said simply, "Yes," and left it at that.

However, Julia pursued her line of thinking further, suggesting that if this were so, then perhaps it should be done in our world and for our world. Just thinking about her words started my body vibrating again. *If I don't do something*, I said to myself, *I'll start shaking uncontrollably again*. We bantered back and forth as to whether I should attempt her suggestion. But in her heart, she made a stronger case than she did with her head, to the point that I finally yielded.

I closed my eyes and completely focused on the scene in the Upper Room. As I focused on Jeshua, he turned and stared at me. He knew what I was about to do, and he smiled in that way only he could smile. A smile that made everything so completely OK that any notion of division or disagreement or judgment fully melted away. My body began to pick up his essence, his love, his compassion, his unadulterated pureness of trust in all that is Divine. Every cell in my body vibrated as if a song of unimaginable beauty ushered forth. The song elevated me beyond the woes and concerns of our world, taking me into a place of wondrous bliss, its sound like a symphony of angelic voices.

"Oh, oh, oh my," I heard Julia say. She had plastered her hands over her ears. "That sound is so piercing, so loud," she said in a forceful voice tinged with fear, snapping me from my reverie once again. Her eyes darted around as if searching for an explanation. "I can't hear," she announced in a concerned but controlled voice. "I can't hear."

What have I done? I asked myself. Immediately I held out my hands offering to ground her, even though she couldn't hear my words. She entrusted her hands to mine. For a few minutes I tried my best to take the vibration from her body and send it into the ground. She shook her head. It wasn't working. Then I began searching for any crystals in the room. After finding a few, I placed them in her hands hoping the crystals might return her hearing by pulling into them whatever had caused her deafness. Again she shook her head. Not working. I strained to come up with a means to undo what had been done, beginning to wonder if I would have to take her to an emergency room or call 911.

My thoughts went back to Jeshua's time, gleaning any kind of experience that would help me figure out how to return Julia's hearing. What I sensed was an event similar to this where what had been done had to be undone. What I saw was a river flowing one way and then flowing back.

Again I reached out for Julia's hands. This time, instead of trying to ground the vibration, I focused on reversing it, returning it to Jeshua with full gratitude and deep appreciation. "OK," she finally said, interrupting my continuing attempt. "The sound is gone from my ears." She looked at me in a way that made me feel like the sorcerer's apprentice. I had ventured where I dare not.

In the most sincere way possible, I tried to apologize but she would have nothing of it. In her wise and compassionate way she repeated the message she conveyed earlier. That Jeshua's mystery, his incredible capacity for love, had to be brought into the world. If I could become that for others, then I must do it. However, a part of me froze unconvinced.

Cheryl looked at me expecting the story to continue. But there was nothing more I wanted to say. The point of my tale was to show her how the Seraphei had gone to great lengths to move her into fully recognizing herself—that part of her that I knew had sheltered all with compassion. In all the years I had known Cheryl, I had never heard her speak a word of malice toward anyone. She avoided drama by responding to it with understanding. She addressed conflict with humble truth, not so she could win the conflict but so the conflict could find common ground as a peaceful choice between the parties. And if the other chose not to enter into peace, then Cheryl always left the other party to sit with their own choice.

"You can't stop there," she insisted. "Who were you?" she demanded with a smile on her face.

"Julia asked me the same question. If I give you the answer you are looking for, it will distort what I'm really trying to tell you. And the reason it will do that is because we are entering a realm where few tread. It's not about who I was. It was about who I became. With my ability, even the hypnosis cannot be looked at in terms that normally are employed. I can't tell you who I was. What I can do is tell you whose eyes I was looking through. I was looking through the eyes of Juda ben Joseph, youngest brother of Jeshua. Some called him Judas Thaddaeus, brother to James, who also was a brother of Jeshua's. In some historical accounts, Juda was also known as Jude of James.

"What you don't understand are the consequences I carry knowing the greatness of a love that passes understanding. Jeshua's capacity to identify himself so completely with the Divine-in-All made him difficult to be around sometimes. It's like coming out of a movie theater at noon. It blinds you. Can you understand how difficult it is to be in a world that thinks love-seeking is a sport or a pursuit of pleasure? As much as I would jump at the chance of falling in love with someone, it never gets very far because I can't and don't start with lust or cultural belief systems about love. Lust is the last piece that fits into the puzzle of love for me. Yet, I can't squander this knowing of divine intimacy that I have that is beyond knowing.

"Our world is at a point where both you and I can no longer rest on hallowed ground like hermits in a cave. In the same way that I must find a way to talk about the supreme love that I have witnessed through the power of becoming, the power of being, so must you find a way to fully embrace your power of being fully who you are. It's that important—to the point that these high celestial beings would go to the trouble of protecting fifty head of heifers just because they can. Just for you. Have you considered what you would have needed to do to care for the herd after the snowstorm? You didn't have feed for them. The grass was covered by a foot of snow.

"The Seraphei were mirrors reflecting back to you how lovingly magnificent this world can be when all of us embrace who we are. At the core, we are like the Seraphei. Truly. At our greatest depths lies our greatest love. Forget about wondering what you are supposed to *do*. After all, we are called 'human beings,' not 'human doings.' Just be completely and wholly who you are. At the center of that lies unconditional love, fathomless compassion, and a light that blinds eyes that have dwelt in darkness."

KNOWING THE UNKNOWN

Cheryl could not rest with not knowing more of what was behind the disappearance of the herd. What we had discussed left her with more questions, and she was a person who needed answers—even if such answers could not be put into words. After spending time chewing on the words we had shared, she decided to get one more point of view. So she asked Sandy if she could connect with the heifers to get "their story." She remembered that Sandy had spent time throughout the summer communicating with the lead heifer whom they called "33" (from the number on her ear tag). Perhaps Sandy could reconnect with 33 and get her version of what had transpired in a similar way Sandy had done many times with the horses. If Sandy could use her connection to 33, as she had done before, to get a view of what the heifer had seen, Cheryl might be able to determine where the herd had been hiding out. She'd witnessed far more unbelievable capabilities in her gifted friend. Certainly the herd could give a better answer than hiding inside a cliff in another dimension.

After calling Sandy, Cheryl waited for her ranch manager to arrive in the great room that overlooked the surrounding landscape. Sandy was just finishing up her evening meal. After cleaning up her utensils, she sat quietly facing Cheryl, a stunning sunset behind her. Cheryl told Sandy nothing of our conversation. She watched as Sandy went into an altered state to connect with 33.

After a couple minutes of concentration, Sandy's voice broke the silence. "I've got her. Let's see. She's saying that she was in a different place than the ranch. Lots of light, but very flat, not bright. There was no water, and she and the rest of the herd were very thirsty. There was some grass around them. She says the herd was confused but not scared. They didn't recognize anything around them. Plus they kept hearing a constant noise." Sandy took a few seconds as she tilted her head, posing as if listening for something. "They didn't know this sound, but as I hear it through 33's ears, it sounds to me like a radio that's not on the right station ... lots-of-static sound with unintelligible voicelike rumbles behind it."

Cheryl's eyes went wide wondering if what I had told her was connected to what Sandy was seeing. "Ask if there were any other creatures in their area."

Sandy communicated the question to 33 by using images. She had learned long ago that forming sentences hindered more than helped in trying to get a notion across to a four-legged. They thought differently than humans. Their world centered around nature, their feet always connected to the earth, which sometimes meant they saw things humans couldn't see. "Wow," said Sandy. "She's showing me very tall, skinny beings that they could see through. The beings were blue, and their legs didn't touch the ground. She was having difficulty understanding why a being didn't touch Mother Earth."

"How did they find their way back?" asked Cheryl.

Sandy put the question to 33 using feelings, centering on the scene just before the herd found its way back to the mineral feeder. She relayed to Cheryl the "exercise of the lost" that she had used during the days the cattle had gone missing, and how she had determined that the "place of finding" would be the mineral feeder. On the fourth day, 33 had seen a hole that opened up to the mineral feeder. At seeing the familiar object, the heifer decided to move through the hole for the nourishment, and the rest of the herd followed.

Upon hearing the description of the blue beings, Cheryl remembered what I had told her about the Seraphei. This information from Sandy reinforced the message I had given. The disappearing heifers meant more than she realized. All information pointed to what I had told her. She now realized that she was wrestling with her own power.

In her pondering, Cheryl recollected passages she had read in one of her favorite books, written by David R. Hawkins, MD, PhD, titled *Power Vs. Force: The Hidden Determinants of Human Behavior* (Veritas

Publishing, 1995). One of the passages addresses how we as humans perceive knowledge and seek it out. As a seeker of knowledge, Cheryl realized that she was limiting herself to an obsolete perception of how knowledge is to be acquired as well as how it is to be perceived:

> This is the pedestrian path of Newtonian physics, based on a limited and limiting view of the world in which all events supposedly happen in an A-B-C sequence. This form of myopia arises from an outdated paradigm of reality. Our wider and far more comprehensive view draws not only upon the essence of the most advanced physics, mathematics and nonlinear theory, but, as well, upon intuitions that can be experientially validated by anyone.

In another passage, Hawkins differentiates the concept of power from that of force in how each shows up in the world, as well as how we are to perceive both. When Cheryl reread this passage, she realized she had to quit looking for answers outside of herself:

> Man thinks he lives by virtue of the forces he can control, but in fact, he's governed by power from unrevealed sources, power over which he has no control. Because power is effortless, it goes unseen and unsuspected. Force is experienced through the senses; power can be recognized only through inner awareness. Man is immobilized in his present condition by his alignment with enormously powerful attractor energy patterns, which he himself unconsciously sets in motion. Moment by moment, he is suspended at this state of evolution, restrained by the energies of force, impelled by the energies of power.

I had discussed with Cheryl on previous occasions how she hides from her power and secrets her gifts. She admitted that because of her tall stature, throughout high school and beyond she was perceived as powerful. In the business world she saw that when she walked into a room she could not go unnoticed. Yet as a young girl she was taught that "children should be seen and not heard," and "Father knows best," from parents who themselves had towed the line in a world that dictated to them what was truth and what was permissible. These people of limit had instilled in her again and again that she was to be a "good girl," knowing her place in a society of the '40s and '50s that dictated how she would become a woman of the '60s.

She continued, "So when I became a widow and needed to fill the space that men had previously filled in my life, everything shifted. I knew I had the capabilities, gifts, and, yes, the power, but I was most reluctant to step into them. Every time I would get close, I would hit a roadblock. I would think, 'There is no way I signed a contract to do ...'"

That's where I stopped her. Power isn't about doing. It's about being.

And that's what I remember most about Jeshua. People forget that he was a rebel, a revolutionary. He didn't care what people thought, and he didn't restrict any aspect of his life or his love, because he was a wild man. His wildness wasn't just in his behavior, it was in his complete ability to trust in himself, and in so doing touch his very core that all of humanity possesses—the Christ within. We have allowed ourselves to be brainwashed into thinking we are not One. Our very cells operate on oneness. Any cell can reproduce an entire body. Our brains contain elements, called monoatomics, which are capable of transforming our thoughts, our messages from the limitations of traveling across nerve tissue, into messages that traverse both time and space, crossing entire galaxies. I have repeatedly demonstrated before audiences and on YouTube that we can innately dwell in dimensions that surpass time and space. And when people see this, their first reaction is one of *fear!*

They think I have power over them. When is humanity going to understanding that we only have power *with* one another, not *over* one another? True power comes only out of Oneness. When I show them how to counteract the consequences of a negative thought or negative suggestion or negative intention by sending out a blessing, they let out a sigh of relief. But then they walk out the door forgetting what has just been shown to them, stepping right back into patterns that diminish them, living by limits they have placed upon themselves. When any one of us is diminished or diminishes another, we all are diminished. So why continue it? In truth, Jeshua showed and proved that no one could diminish him. And as strongly as I know this and have experienced it, I still have one last "enemy" to conquer in that regard. I have to stop choosing to diminish myself. I must constantly choose to be the complete me. And in so doing, I can give to others what Jeshua always gave to me— Love that passes understanding.

Chapter 9

BEYOND BELIEF

Zak and I continued our comedic tug of war: I kept insisting that all he was seeking was to be found within, while he kept insisting that I was keeping information from him that would hasten his spiritual journey. He reminded me of myself years ago when I would quote one of my favorite sayings, "Lord, grant me patience, only give it to me now." In Zak's case it was "Allah, grant me awareness, and why don't I have it already?"

America is a society of the instantaneous. We eat fast foods that aren't healthy for us, we place unrealistic deadlines on ourselves and others that stress us to an early grave, and we take pills that had better make us feel better before the sun sets or somebody's going to hear about it. Nevermind the studies that show that pharmaceuticals are one of the leading causes of death. Zak was a product of his surroundings and the belief systems that had made him successful. He was now striving to "succeed" as a spiritual being, and as far as he was concerned he didn't care if that was to be found in a drug, or a seminar, or a fortune cookie—he wanted awareness, and he wanted it now.

I was the latest curiosity, and no matter how much he wanted what he perceived that I had, I would not, could not hand over that which was uniquely me. He had to find his wonder within.

In my work with the Quantum Generation, I operated under the Jungian notion that it is not the purpose of the individual to serve the community, it is the purpose of the community to serve the individual. Jung differentiated between the "individual," "individuality," and "the individuation process."

In his work "The Structure of the Unconscious," Jung states the following:

> A distinction must be made between individuality and the individual. The individual is determined on the one hand by the principle of uniqueness and distinctiveness, and on the other by the society to which he belongs. He is an indispensable link in the social structure.... The individual is precisely that which can never be merged with the collective and is never identical with it.

Jung further differentiates between individuality and individuation in "The Function of the Unconscious":

> Individualism means deliberately stressing and giving prominence to some supposed peculiarity rather than to collective considerations and obligations. But individuation means precisely the better and more complete fulfillment of the collective qualities of the human being, since adequate consideration of the peculiarity of the individual is more conducive to a better social performance than when the peculiarity is neglected or suppressed.

In spite of my efforts to convince Zak that success could no longer be attained by bowing to acquired belief systems or societal norms, he seemed baffled by the notion that I saw within him a tremendous gift, what Jung called "peculiarity." This peculiar and unique ability made him outstanding but he wanted me to prove to him or give to him the magic potion that would make what he saw as outstanding—me and my peculiarities—his.

At one point he started a new business alongside his commercial real estate business—Vedic astrology—a significant departure from the belief systems he had held when first we met. Interestingly, he decided that if he combined holodynamics with astrology, clients might be better and more uniquely served. I thought it to be a wonderful idea. He asked if I would sit in on some of his sessions with clients to make sure that he didn't miss any of the principles of the holodynamics. We agreed on a fee, and I sat in on four different sessions, each one more amazing than the previous. What I was seeing in his office convinced me he had found a winner of a skill that would help others in ways I would never be able to. I couldn't stop grinning watching how skillfully he combined the principles of astrology with the archetypal counterparts in holodynamics. After each session I would make pointers how he could more deeply explore the path that the holodyne was taking him. I made a point as well to show him how effective his work had been. At the end of our last team session, he confessed to me that he felt insecure in his practice. His edict: "I can't match you in how well you work with the holodynes, how well you understand the symbols." Exasperated, I enunciated to him that I had been using holodynamics for five years. He had only jumped into it five weeks ago. Yet he could not get past comparing himself to me and gave up what I considered a uniquely magnificent practice. I could only shake my head.

With enduring admiration I continued to consult for Zak with regard to his real estate investments and management. His partners had just purchased a strip mall for a bargain price because the previous owner had been clobbered by growing restrictions of the banking system after the stock market crash of 2008. He was having particular trouble renting out one area of the complex and decided I should take a look at it.

With dowsing rods in hand, I moved from section to section through the empty rooms, coming to a stop in what had to have been the data processing center. Cables lay strewn everywhere. "This place is dead," I announced.

A smile crept across Zak's handsome face, his eyes twinkling. "What do you mean dead? How can a place be dead?"

"There's no chi in here, no life force. It's stagnant ... dead."

We had worked together enough for him to accept my explanation. "Can you fix it?"

"First I have to find out why there's no chi. And I can't do it in here because my dowsing rods won't work. I'm going to have to step into the area next to the front door." Which I did. Watching the dowsing rods swing back and forth, Zak asked me to say my questions aloud. His understanding of how I discovered information allowed him to participate in my efforts, sometimes thinking of question I hadn't considered.

"Well now I know why this place won't rent," I announced. "Karma."

A chuckle bubbled up from Zak's throat. "How can karma affect renting?"

"Happens quite often," I offered. "I see it all the time. In this case, the previous renter had cheated a lot of people. Badly. My information points to what was the computer center. He was probably cooking the books to avoid bankruptcy. And a lot of people suffered because of it. So what I need to do is use a combination of blessing and sound to change the vibration in here."

"This I gotta see," Zak declared.

I raised my hands in the air and called in the angels that assist me in such matters, sending out blessings to all who had been affected because of the previous renter's fear of failing, fear of truth, fear of punishment. With intent I expressed that all aspects of fear be replaced by appreciation for lessons learned, and forgiveness for abandoning the divine aspects of himself. I then expressed sincerity that whoever should next occupy this space would replace the trauma that had resulted from dishonesty and trepidation with healing and comfort.

Next, I retrieved one my tuning forks that rings with a specific frequency given to us by the angelic realm. I picked several locations where I would ring the tuning fork and place it on glass or wood or metal so that the structure would pick up the vibrations along with the intent that this space would no longer hold the vibrations of negativity, but the vibrations of blessing for all concerned. When I had finished, I looked at Zak, and, after checking my dowsing rods, announced, "The place should rent now. What I think would be best is that someone in the healing arts occupy this space. So if a chiropractor or a dentist or massage therapist comes your way, bring them here. They should resonate with what I have done here."

In a matter of days, a dentist showed up looking for new space. Zak called me.

"OK, how did you do that?" he started out, wanting to understand how karma, blessings, and a tuning fork could change a space to the point that it would rent after sitting idle for months.

I cited the work done by Dr. William Tiller, as described in Lynne McTaggart's book, *The Intention Experiment* (Free Press, 2008), where the esteemed scientist discovered he had somehow profoundly altered quantum realities "in the very fabric of physical reality." McTaggart follows up Tiller's work with that of researcher Graham Watkins and his wife Anita as well as the research done by biologist Bernard Grad at McGill University in Montreal, Canada.

In Graham's work regarding what is affectionately labeled the "mouse-ether effect," he recruited human participants known for their psychic abilities, to work with mice that had been placed under anesthesia. He asked the psychics to mentally attempt to hasten the recovery time of the mice. The results proved significant. In fact, the more they repeated the experiments (seven times) the more significant the recovery time, as opposed to the control mice who had to recover on their own.

But what proved baffling was what happened afterwards. A new group of mice was put under anesthesia and then placed in the same space where the previous group of mice had been worked on by the psychic participants. Even though the participants were no longer present, the new mice still recovered more quickly than the control group. The results indicate that a lingering effect on reality had remained.

I tried to explain to Zak that I had also discovered that I could alter the "reality" of space using blessings or sacred oils or tuning forks of special frequencies. And that the effect of the change lingered. That's how the rental space had been altered. I explained to him how I had discovered that two great wheels determine how reality can be influenced: the Wheel of Karma and the Wheel of Grace. What determines which of the two wheels will roll across a reality are humans. We are that miraculous in our ability to determine what will show up in reality. We can choose to live in realities determined by karma (usually influenced by belief systems), or we can choose to live in realities determined by grace (the essence of Divine Love). If we choose to bless a situation or a person or a thing, we take it with us into the Wheel of Grace. In the Wheel of Grace, all karma is transformed by the oneness of love. Divine Love may and can be called forth from us at any time we choose. We just have to choose.

183

"Teach me how to do this," he demanded.

I started laughing. How many times did I have to tell him? "It's easy," I insisted. "Just be yourself. Fully embrace who you are."

"What if I don't know who I am? You seem to know who I am better than I do. What's the secret? How do I create this Wheel of Grace?"

After acknowledging that what Zak was really doing was trying to get me to help him give up one more belief system, I began to explain why all the Ascended Masters who had walked the earth always said the same thing: We live in an illusion. Or maya. How we walk in these illusions is determined by choosing either the Wheel of Karma or the Wheel of Grace. It's not to imply that karma is bad and grace is good. That's not the case. Each has its place: each has its unique ability. Living in karma is like deciding that one is going to place a cast around a broken bone. There is pain, there is discomfort, but the bone mends. However, it does more than mend. The place where the break had occurred is actually stronger than before. It is much less prone to break in that area again.

Grace works differently. With grace, one may choose to move the broken bone back to a reality of wholeness. Think of it as moving the bone back to the past before the break occurred, or to an alternate future where the break never occurred in the first place. But the bone is once again whole—restored. However, this choosing makes the bone just as vulnerable as it was previous to the break. In essence, the reality may have been shifted or changed, but the bone remains the same—unlike with karma.

When Zak had asked me to influence the condition of the office rental space that wasn't renting, I chose to move the space into a place of grace. The Wheel of Grace removed the influence of the Wheel of Karma. However, knowing the permanency that karma can instill in a given situation (the mended broken bone), I set the intent that Zak try to rent the space to someone from the healing arts so that a "new" karma would move into place, serving both the future renter and Zak, who would realize continued revenue from renters who might follow afterward ... or who might rent nearby. I knew that he had other spaces that needed renting in the strip mall. By using the Wheel of Karma after using the Wheel of Grace, surrounding influence came into play. And sure enough, before long, the entire mall was rented. All had been well served: Zak, the renters, the surrounding space itself, along with myself (who had been paid well for my work, and would be consulted again).

Nonetheless, Zak wanted more. He wanted to be able to do what I had done. He still wanted to walk a path that I tread upon. How was I ever going to get him to realize that he had his own path? A path with unique and wonderful purpose. I decided to tell him about a part of myself that I had seen in him.

THE STORY OF TWO LIVES

In the book *Indigo Rising: Awakening the Powers of the Children of the New Earth* (DreamSpeaker Creations, 2005), I describe how I came down with an incurable disease. I ended up being cured of the disease after the appearance of an angel during a hypnosis session, with the angel continuing to appear to me for the next three years. But the reason the angel had appeared in the first place stemmed from the therapist's proposing the simple challenge, "Let us find the cause of this disease." Simple, no? Not really.

What ended up happening under hypnosis was my being taken back to a past life where I had been a cathedral architect in seventeenth century France, not far from the border with Germany at that time. My fame was reflected by the great number of students who came to apprentice with me, learning how to combine different forms of architecture into a beauty that provided more than just good structure. However, I was also a rebel, highly critical of how the Church had burdened humanity with its sense of what was right and what was wrong, what was sacred and what was profane. And to express my rebellion with how the Church had made aspects of love ugly and sinful, I secretly built into my works statements of satire. In this particular city, where I had fallen in love with the meister's (mayor's) daughter, that satire lay hidden in the rain gutters off the cathedral roofing. Even during the Age of Discovery, the Age of Revolution, did I rail against belief systems.

I had it made. Wealth. Status. Love. That was, until one regretful day when a severe thunderstorm blanketed the area in darkness, dumping sheets of rain upon the city, making it possible for townspeople to see the gutters in all their glory during daylight hours. The flashing lightning cast the gutters in shadow in such a way that my secret was revealed, showing the carved angels, serving as downspouts, to also be large penises taking a whiz off the top of the cathedral. The scandal spread near and far.

The bishop ordained that I be shunned, ostracized, which during those times was close to getting a death sentence. Anyone who feared the power of the Church would not dare speak to or associate with me. I lost everything. But the worst was losing my beloved fiancée, who was escorted off to Italy, never to see me again. My reaction was to drown my sorrows, eventually becoming a town drunk. I could have risen to the challenge and championed the young architectural students across Europe who loved what I had done—that I had dared to take on the ugly side of the Church with its ability to label any aspect of love as sinful. But I didn't. I had lost my precious love. She meant everything to me. And without her, I saw myself as worthless, slowly killing myself with drink.

My life ended one night while riding a borrowed horse, drunk out of my mind, when I suddenly clotheslined myself with a tree limb that knocked my body into a ravine next to a graveyard, my neck having been broken. Those who found me thought me dead, not realizing that I had been paralyzed, barely able even to breath. Because I had been ostracized, I could not be buried on hallowed ground. So they buried me where I lay. Alive.

While under the hypnosis, I watched as the dirt slowly covered me and suffocated my last breath. My daring to be myself and go against the establishment had snuffed me out. It was after this memory that the therapist took me into the afterlife where the angel appeared. As the therapist asked questions, the angel began to respond using my voice. When the therapist discovered that he was talking to an angel, he delved into how and why this was transpiring, asking why the disease now afflicted me.

What the angel revealed was that I had failed to live the life I had come to live. In deep contrast to the life of the architect, in this life I had towed the line by never challenging belief systems or the voices of authority. The karma of the architect still weighed upon my soul. So, in this life, rather than confront belief systems that did not honor me or support me or empower me, I had repressed who I was, always trying to be the "good boy." In the process, I had completely compromised not only who I was meant to be in this current world, I had caused my body to resort to an incurable disease to force me to deal with my self-imprisonment. It was now slowly killing me in similar fashion to each spadeful of dirt that had suffocated the paralyzed architect.

After the therapist had brought me out of the hypnotic trance, the angel remained, continuing to talk to me in front of the psychologist as I fell into a weeping fit, seeing what I had done to myself in this lifetime. The therapist could not see the angel, even though he had conversed with it earlier in the session. He watched helplessly as I moved into traumatic realization that I had enslaved myself with belief systems that I had allowed to be placed upon me by others. The specter of once again becoming an outcast by the world around me kept me from embracing the Jungian notion of seeing myself as an individual. And because of that, I was unable to surround myself with a social structure (community) that would empower me into individuation. Not only was I lesser as a human being for this, but so was the world I had been born into made lesser.

A little over twenty-four hours after the appearance of the angel, the incurable disease left me, never to return. However, I struggled emotionally for three more years as I learned to let go of the Wheel of Karma, later to embrace the Wheel of Grace—a process that took me seven more years to complete.

KNOWING THE ULTIMATE UNKNOWN

Zak finally began to get the picture as to why I kept insisting that he find his power, his answers, and his miracles within himself. Slowly he began giving up the temptations of "instant spirituality" and "short-cut awareness." When any of us pursue such temptations, we find ourselves seeking approval by elements of an I-want-what-you-have culture. As Jung rightly points out, the only way to individuation is to find the peculiar within oneself. Seeking approval by others will not bring about this self-discovery. Indeed, one must find fellow renegades who will support this vision quest into the peculiar, or one must self-initiate.

Zak was not the only person who came to me sporting the "instant" syndrome. Almost every young person of the Quantum Generation who has sought me out has whined consistently, "I just want to be normal. Why can't I be normal?" This is destruction-by-belief-system at its worst. When a kid grows up in an instant-based society, that kid expects most of life to be had with a push of a button or a taking of a pill or a purchase at a Jiffy Mart. Individuation cannot be bought. The peculiar cannot be found by seeking "normal." Pursuit of the normal can only sabotage individuation in the worst way, as in my case with an incurable disease.

In my work with late-teens and twenty-somethings, I have found my most effective means of bringing them into healing and wholeness is to hold up a mirror to them. Instead of becoming the Knight of the Mirrors, as in the Broadway musical *The Man of La Mancha,* where Don Quixote dies from being forced to see that he is nothing but a crazy old man, I became the Phantom of the Mirror showing the person seeking my help that the individual is the Healer, the Magician, the King or Queen, the Warrior, or the Hierophant—that the individual is the Gate-keeper of the Divine-Within. Then, in true Jungian fashion, I found that the individual could return to the world not as an outcast but as a bearer of sacred gift—the Self.

Because the world has moved to a level of greater awareness, I no longer work with the Zaks of our world. I no longer handle real estate as a metaphor for transformation, nor do I have any pretense that I can teach the Quantum Generation any longer. They now have become the teachers, the leaders, the voices calling us into fullness.

As much as I know that the individual must be recognized, empowered, and initiated into "being," I aso know full well that each of us as individuals is a living quantum paradox—we are also One. We have only to look around to see that Nature honors and respects this paradox. Biologists know full well that whales (cetaceans in general) can operate as a pod, united not only in movement but also in mind, or they can operate as individuals. When you observe a pod of whales lazily rising and submerging on the surface, they most likely are in sleep mode. What biologists have discovered is that all their brains are linked as if they are one mind. Humans can do the same. In a study conducted at the Department of Neuroscience at Mount Sinai School of Medicine in New York, scientists found that cetacean brains and human brains are amazingly similar, even to the point where we possess a counterpart to their echolocation. Other studies show that some whales actually possess the same neurons found in the human brain (*The Journal of Comparative Neurology*, 2009).

Jung makes it clear that the "peculiar" individual's greatest benefit is found in that individual's ability to make society as a whole "more conducive to a better social performance." In other words, uniqueness of the individual fosters betterment for our society as whole. Perhaps we should then look more closely at that "whole."

In Lynne McTaggart's book, *The Bond: Connection Through the Space Between Us* (Free Press, 2011), she describes continuing research that takes Bruce Lipton's findings—that we are not our genes—even further. Lipton deftly points out that it is our environment and receptor switches on our cell walls that determine our genetic traits. McTaggart cites several sources that cause her to conclude that the greatest environmental influence in our genetic makeup as an individual is one another.

Giacomo Rizzolatti, a neurologist at the University of Parma in Italy, discovered that within the brains of humans there is no distinction between observation and action. In other words, we are what we watch. But it doesn't end there. In the process of observing, we become the other. "We understand the actions of others by simulating the entire experience from a personal vantage point, as though it were happening to us," states McTaggart. "When you see someone smile or grimace, as far as your brain is concerned it is you who are happy or disturbed" (*BMC Neuroscience* 10, 2009).

Such findings place even more emphasis on Jung's statement that it is key for the individual to enter into "uniqueness and distinctiveness," because each and every one of us is "an indispensable link in the societal structure."

McTaggart concludes that Rizzolatti's discovery has far more impact than what our world presently realizes. She hammers that home in the following:

> Rizzolatti's discovery has now been universally acknowledged as a remarkable advance in our understanding of how the brain processes the actions and emotions of others. Less recognized, however, are the enormous implications of his discovery of the biology of perception and social interaction. As his work makes clear, perceiving the world is not an individual affair, limited to our own mental capacities, but a process involving shared neural circuitry. We internalize the experience of others at every moment, automatically and immediately, without conscious effort, using a neural shorthand created of our own experience. In the very act of connecting with someone, even on the most superficial level, we are involved in a relationship of the utmost intimacy. Our understanding of the complexities of our world occurs through the constant melding of the observer with the observed.

The significance of all this is far greater than anyone may realize. We see that implication in actions from the angelic realm. Starting in 1997, these beings began providing information about what they call "the Well of Souls." These wells create a quantum condition of linking beyond what Jung cited. The angelic realm stated that the Jungian condition did not end with linking one human being to the society as a whole, but went even further in establishing a link with the heavenly as well. The angels provided an elaborate set of rituals that set up this Well of Souls connection not only to seven human beings with seven distinct gifts ("uniqueness and distinctiveness"), but the angels also went to great lengths to show how these seven gifts are mirrored by angelic counterparts, and how the seven move into Oneness (*On the Wings of Heaven*, DreamSpeaker Creations, 1999). And once the Oneness has been experienced, then each of the seven goes and finds seven more to continue the spreading of the Well of Souls.

While conducting a summer workshop in Chicago, I showed the audience the mind-boggling potentials when humans decide to work in Oneness with coherent intent. After explaining the seven archetypes the angels had given as a means of finding one's gift, and thereby moving into individuation, I had them move into their seven groups as a means of letting them see a mirror of this aspect of themselves. Then I showed them how they could take their archetypes (using the seven colors of the rainbow as a metaphor) and move into sacred geometric positions. I let them take turns standing in the middle of the geometry:

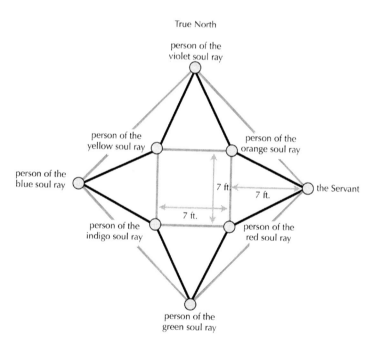

Once everyone understood the mechanics of this angelic information, I then instructed them how to use their Oneness in altering quantum realities by demonstrating such change through a volunteer. A woman stepped forward who expressed her intent—that she would like to regain her hearing. None of us knew she was deaf because her lipreading skills had allowed her to work with the group without signing. I showed the audience how to create an elemental using their collective consciousness, in this case a new inner ear. They accomplished this by being shown a picture of a healthy inner ear from Grey's Anatomy (the workshop was in an air-conditioned library meeting room). I then had all of them collectively imagine placing a new, healthy inner ear into both ears of the deaf woman, making sure we had no expectation of what the result might be, other than whatever showed up would serve the highest and best purpose of this woman.

Afterward, the woman returned to her place, and those who had participated in the formation continued to hold the intent for another twenty minutes. At about the fifteen-minute mark, the deaf woman screamed, shocking us all from our meditative state. She had both hands clasped against her ears. "What is that? What is that?" she kept saying over and over again. She looked terribly disturbed.

One of the people close to her moved in front of her face so she could lip-read and asked, "Tell us what is happening. So we can help. What's happening."

"Oh, dear God," said the deaf woman gasping. "I can hear you. But what is that terrible sound?"

All of us looked at one another with blank looks. What could she possibly be hearing that the rest of us could not hear? The helper asked the woman to describe the noise. The woman responded using her voice to make a growling-like sound, as if trying to imitate thunder, tears streaming down her face.

One of the other participants volunteered, "Oh, I know what she's hearing. I bet it's the air conditioning!"

Once the air-conditioning cycled off, the woman removed her hands from her ears. Looking around at everyone, gratitude pouring from her eyes, she choked out, "Thank you, everyone. Dear Lord, I can hear." The audience sat soberly silent with the obvious surprise showing on their faces. What have we done? their faces shone. And with "we," they didn't mean just themselves. The evidence was staring right back at them.

In a similar incident that occurred at an Edmonton, Alberta expo, I conducted a workshop on the Well of Souls. Because there wasn't a person to represent each angelic archetype (or soul ray), I had to use precious stones that held the vibration of the missing soul ray to complete the geometry of the angelic gateway, or Gate of Grace. These are terms used by the angels to describe the same geometry used in different ways. Because of time constraints, I wasn't able to include a section on creating elementals with consciousness. There was only one volunteer who would go into the middle of the Well of Souls. When I asked her to sit in the middle of the Well of Souls, she kvetched, "I'm not a good person for this. I don't believe in this stuff. I came mostly out of curiosity." Experience has taught me that those who are open with their skepticism are often open to results as well (though sometimes after the fact). I decided to stick with the skeptic.

I said to her, "There's no pressure here. We aren't placing any expectations on you, nor will we have any attachments as to the outcome. We will simply choose to support you in your intent, and let the angels do the rest in concert with the rest of us here." The look on her face was one of don't-say-I-didn't-warn-you as she carefully sat on the floor in the midst of the other participants who had stepped into the geometric formation.

After demonstrating how humans can enter into the state of Oneness, I instructed those of the different gifts (the different soul rays, the different angelic archetypes) to support the intent of the woman centered in the sacred geometric formation. When asked if she would like to share her intent with those who would support her, the volunteer declined, saying she'd prefer to keep it to herself. On her head she sported an unusual hat, her hair tucked up underneath. Her eyes showed a blush of embarrassment.

After checking my dowsing rods, I affirmed that the woman's helping angel was, indeed, present, as were the angels connecting to the Well of Souls. I instructed the others to simply set their intent to be in alignment with the volunteer. Everyone entered into a meditative state holding the intent of the skeptical woman in the middle.

At the end of fifteen minutes, I thanked everyone and then looked to the women in the center to see if there was anything she wanted to share. She began moving her arms as if she were trying to squirm out of a tight sweater. Her hands raised up about the level of her forehead.

Excitement flooded her face. At this time, she informed the rest of us that she was afflicted with frozen shoulder syndrome, a painful condition that can lead to paralysis. Doctors don't understand what brings it on. Usually it's an injury that later brings in the unexplainable virus that starts the paralysis process. I've had it myself in both my shoulders, and had to undergo extensive physical therapy, which sometimes doesn't work. In my case, it did. And thankfully so, because I was in the process of losing the use of my arms.

"This is the highest I've been able to raise my arms in a long time," said the delighted volunteer. After checking my dowsing rods again, I encouraged the woman to ask her angel to assist her some more. I could see her skepticism waning. Once again, everyone went quiet. After about a ten-minute period, I checked one more time. I asked the volunteer to again test her range of motion—perhaps she could reach the back of her head.

Then slowly she edged her hands up to her hat, lifting it from her head as high as she could. She then lowered the hat into her lap and began to weep fully. As her tears rushed down her cheeks, she kept patting her hair as if to arrange it into place, softly mewling, "My hair, my hair." Over and over again she would touch her hair and, in between sobs, softly cry out, "My hair, I can touch my hair." A few minutes later she explained, "I haven't been able to comb my hair for six months." Those in the Well of Souls stood stunned watching her. They had no idea what was transpiring.

Once she calmed down some, the tearful woman announced to everyone, "I'm sorry, you must be wondering what has happened. For six months I haven't been able to raise my hands above my chest. I've always been fond of my hair. I used to comb it all the time each night. One to two hundred strokes a night. It always soothed me. But when I got the frozen shoulder, I was no longer able to comb my hair. I couldn't even wash it or set it myself. The only time my hair got combed was if someone did it for me." Tears began to fall afresh. "I felt too embarrassed to go out in public unless my hair was presentable, so I started wearing hats. Any of you who know me, see me all the time wearing a hat to cover my hair. I didn't want people to see my hair unsightly. And now I am able to touch my hair. I will be able to comb it again. It used to bring me such joy. And now I can have that joy again." Her tears erupted into streams, her voice choking out, "Thank you, everyone. Thank you, angels, thank you, thank you. This is a miracle."

There wasn't a dry eye in the place, including yours truly. The scene hit everyone powerfully, the once-skeptic continuing to cry for joy throughout the rest of the workshop. Even years afterward, I still hear from folks who attended that workshop and remember the role they had played in the manifestation of a miracle by entering with the angels into the Oneness of the Well of Souls.

McTaggart's findings that we are one with whomever we observe can now extend into the heavens. And if our linking capabilities go into the heavens, the question must then be asked, "Where does it end?" And the honest answer is that it doesn't.

In 2008, the angelic appearances with Joseph Crane reached a crest. The angels indicated a critical point was about to ensue—but only if humanity could gather 444 people into a sacred geometric formation that would thereby link all of humanity with the angelic hosts. What humanity would then begin to see would be the "first vibrations of peace," a new kind of peace—what ancient traditions called the Golden Age of Peace. The first vestiges of this peace would be the end of the insanity of world leaders who used war as a means to an end on our planet.

Those over the years who had already entered the Well of Souls in large numbers stepped into action by creating what was then called "The Gathering of One." This event had two parts: (1) those who would come together to make up the sacred 444 geometry at West Yellowstone, Montana, and (2) those around the world who also would enter into specified sacred geometry that would connect to the central group at Yellowstone. This ended up involving some 30,000 people from every continent on Earth, including Antarctica.

As an aside, I must address why this event became so powerful and so key as a critical point for humanity. In the movie *What the Bleep Do We Know!?*, which can still be rented, there are wonderful scenes in which Roger Nelson, PhD, and Dean Radin, PhD, are interviewed, commenting about the Washington, DC, experiment in which the crime rate there dropped by twenty-five percent. This was accomplished by bringing into coherence 4,000 people who together set the intent that the crime rate would fall by that specific percentage that summer. It did. In fact, normally the crime rate elevates some twenty-five percent in summer, which it didn't. Both Nelson and Radin became involved in the Global Consciousness Project, which began exploring the effects of coherent consciousness and its influence on global reality.

The effectiveness of altering crime-rate realities by focusing on a single city is one matter. Setting an intent and focusing on the entire globe is quite another. Yet that is what the angelic realm asked humanity to do in June 2008. Please note that the number the angels said would work was 444 people, not 4,000, which had been used for Washington, DC. How could a magnitude smaller have greater effect on a body of reality magnitudes larger? Sacred geometry coupled with coherent intent, that's how. When 444 human beings entered into sacred geometric formation using the Well of Souls, that sacred formation linked those 444 with the heavenly hosts. In so doing, the number of coherent souls holding intent jumped wildly.

Since the Gathering of One, many have noted that we still have war. However, I would point out that wars between nations have steadily decreased, and that the old wars are finally winding down. I would also submit that those despots and leaders who have fomented war in the past, are falling from power. But what is more important to note is that which did not appear in any media.

After the Gathering of One, the angelic realm once again asked humanity to enter into sacred geometric formations—on September 28 and October 12, 2008. On the day after each of those events happened, the U.S. stock market collapsed. This signaled the beginning of the end of greed-based economics. Entire books can be written, and have, as to what happened behind the scenes, and whether the corrupt banking system that is partnered with the military-industrial complex is in the throes of collapse. As the truth ultimately reveals itself, as it must do, the world will discover that the angels exhorted us to alter our global reality through global consciousness because humanity was at the precipice of utter destruction, the kind of destruction that can only be comprehended by using the word "apocalyptic."

At some point, our world will discover what I already know—that on October 7, 2008, Biblical prophecy moved out of our quantum reality, leading each of us, and the world that we chose to co-create, into becoming the New Eden. The world as we once knew it has moved into a parallel timeline, while we have entered a new timeline. That new timeline has at its foundation the New Eden, the New Paradise. This the angelic realm has verified.

All that humanity has to do is open the gates and walk in. How do we do that? By each and every one of us fully embracing the unique, the wonderful, the "peculiar," and the distinctive in ourselves. In so doing, we can then have complete quantum entanglement with the whole, the One. The Gateway to the One rests within each individual. Let all of us step into that place. With unconditional love, let all of us step into the ultimate unknown—ourselves.

A thousand blessings to you all.

May you trust yourselves in the new journey that is you.

Spread Peace that passes understanding by becoming Peace.

Embrace Love.

Dance with Joy as you uncover the Great Mystery that is you.

EPILOGUE

Several have asked what happened with Zak, Jesse, Jake, and Cheryl beyond what I told in the book. Many others asked how I ever got into shamanic real estate, which makes me laugh when I think of it. Rather than repeating these stories over and over, I decided to provide a wrap-up as the epilogue.

Zak went through a major transformation after working with me. His first step to self-empowerment occurred through his studying of qi gong. From there he developed his interests in yoga to such a degree as to become a yoga teacher. In the discipline and self-exploration of yoga, he realized its potential to bring ancient wisdom and modern awareness into a harmony of exercise and a spiritual pursuit that goes beyond the individual, to tap into the synergistic power of a group or community (think Well of Souls). Out of that is growing a lotuslike outreach where yoga takes the Buddha-Within (namasté) and extends outward to coalesced or cohesive consciousness to the Buddha-in-All. Think of it as the lotus being not only the beautiful blossom that unfolds on the surface of the pond but also the stem and roots that reach into the world, the earth, the mud of the pond that nourishes life. This new system of yoga seeks to strengthen the mind and the spirit, as well as the body, through gifts found in each and every one of us. It's a daring step but an important step, not only for Zak and Elizabeth, but to all us who see life as an opportunity for growth rather than a burden to endure.

Jesse became an adept healer, eventually joining the organization of Her Holiness Sai Maa, a guru and leader who formed Humanity in Unity, located in Boulder, Colorado. Jesse quickly rose to a place of prominence and regard as he continued his journey in self-awareness. To this day he will call me out of the blue just to touch base and show respect to one who first saw his giftedness as a blessing to the world. My days with him left me speechless at times and devastated at others. The stories around our short sojourn together is enough to fill another book, which I have already started. It took ten years before I felt I could write *A World Beyond Belief*, knowing how difficult it would be for people to entertain the truth of it. Another five years may transpire before I speak of the breathtaking encounters with Jesse. In one night on a sacred mountain, he accomplished more than I did in the first fifty years of my life. That one night is something I almost never talk about. But perhaps the world is more ready than I realize.

Like Jesse, Jake's story is a "life beyond belief." My thoughts are to take their adventures and write them as fiction. For sometimes the truth is stranger than fiction—too strange for folks to embrace. Jake's life is not limited to this planet. He has dropped on my plate more than once a sumptuous feast of information that not even our most talented scientists can comprehend. The question remains as to what I should do with this miraculous information. His gift is walking between the worlds while mine is serving as the scribe of the heavens and the otherworlds. Each time he has dared to dip his big toe into the river we call life, people try to make him out to be beyond human. Unfortunately that goes against everything he stands for. His day will come when he will show many the magic of the human condition, the wonder of being masters who have been made to forget their wonder. Frankly, around him I've had to get used to the startling evidence of objects, from meteorite stones to thumb drives containing files directing me to information I would not otherwise have found, showing up out of nowhere as well as disappearing at the most annoying times. Has this been only to get my attention? Or has it been to prepare me to tell the world that we, dear and glorious people, are the stuff of stars (as Carl Sagan loved saying so often)? Stay tuned.

Cheryl continues her role as the guardian over sacred land. Her friendship alone is the single greatest comfort I know, for she has no fear of the unknown. Never do I feel alone when the unexplainable addresses me either most rudely or most wondrously, for she always lends an ear. She has the ability to comprehend the incomprehensible. I love the fact that she is my only friend who has had a longstanding subscription to *Scientific American*, oftentimes sending me articles that give credence to some of the more mind-boggling aspects of my life. She is still visited by the Seraphei Seraphim, who know far more than I what her most likely role is in a world beyond belief. For the day will come when she will be able to tell the many how marvelous it is to be human, how blessed we are to inherit a new world that we shall all co-create.

The one person I wish I could have included in my tales is a man named Tep. In my younger years, Tep went to great lengths to pry me out of my shell. I never knew how red my face could get until I met him. On warm Portland nights, we would enter into conversations that made the world seem like a feast to behold instead of a terror from which to shrink. Tep would ask me things no one had ever asked, such as "What do you think Peggy is doing with her latest man-beast right now?" Peggy (not her real name) was a glutton for life. She pursued relationships the way some people hunt for four-leaf clovers, fingers rummaging through the richness of a lawn rather than waiting patiently, cranelike, for one to pop up out of the grass. When I told Tep what I thought she was doing, he would laugh in a hyena frenzy, wondering where I had found such an imagination. However, when he discovered the truth a few days later, he began to wonder about me and ask more questions. From there he began asking me about his own life and where it was to lead. One night, he stated bluntly, "You know, you really have a gift there. You should hang out your shingle." Of course I told him he was crazy.

Tep was not a man to be put aside. He began organizing parties in which he would invite friends over—the condition being that they had to wear sneakers. Unbeknownst to me he secretly plotted to have me display my abilities of psychometry. After a few drinks ... OK, not so few ... he pulled off one of his sneakers, inviting everyone to "Watch this!" He then handed me his sneaker and asked me to tell his future from holding the sneaker. Never did I realize I could be so outrageously funny, so entertaining. From that night on, I was a hit with his friends. For a while, one of Tep's favorite pastimes was to organize a sneaker party. He had to stop because so many were showing up that the neighbors began to complain.

Once again he entreated me to "hang out my shingle." The idea of asking people to pay me money to tell them information I thought blatantly obvious seemed criminal. Not to be hindered any further, Tep asked me what I would be willing to take in trade for my doing another reading for him. Tep was a prediction slut. He couldn't get enough. "What do you truly enjoy that you would take in trade?"—thinking that I might ask for clothes or books or a bottle of Galliano (Harvey Wallbangers were big in those days).

With Tep's not taking no for an answer, I thought deeply about my response. "Junior Mints," I concluded. "I'd trade you a reading for a box of Junior Mints." Honestly, I really loved Junior Mints. Tep burst out laughing. He tried to get me to up the price but it was Junior Mints or nothing.

That was my first professional act as a seer. For months my exchange for readings rested on boxes of Junior Mints. I eventually became sick of them. Tep then asked me to graduate to something of greater value. Because I had moved to Montana by this time, I lacked one delicacy I could no longer find. So I asked him to send me jars of Nalley Valley Tartar Sauce. Then it became boxes of Nalley's Tartar Sauce. And finally, I begrudgingly let Tep talk me into actually taking cash in recompense. That changed my professional life, and the way I looked at myself. No longer did I see myself as a hoodwink but as a blessing to those who would become my clients. When I became a *New York Times* bestselling author, I sent Tep my first book. His sublime craziness had swooped me from my nerdy, isolated world into my initiation into self-awareness. I will bless him always. For without him, I do not believe I would have ever discovered that this life is a world beyond belief.

ABOUT THE AUTHOR

GW HARDIN is a *New York Times* bestselling author, having written or co-written eight books having to do with true stories about the extraordinary. Hardin specializes in the bringing together of opposite worlds, using science and scientific research as a backdrop to his unexplainable stories. He is one of the foremost authorities on the angelic realm while also writing about the parallels that quantum physics has to meta-messages from non-ordinary sources. He can speak about angelic gateways in one breath and turn  around and display matching patterns used in the quantum Theory of Everything M8 Model.

As a lecturer, GW Hardin has presented talks at colleges and universities around the country and has given many keynote addresses at conferences. He has appeared numerous times on television and radio shows that have reached millions of people. These days he is working on a new book that explores the bridging of the worlds of the extraordinary to applications in everyday life.

The author has appeared on radio and television, and has been interviewed in magazines and newspapers across the nation. A graduate in mathematics at the University of Washington, starting his career as a computer scientist, he is presently working to create New Consciousness outreach programs across the globe.

CPSIA information can be obtained at www.ICGtesting.com
Printed in the USA
BVOW070739050412

286929BV00001B/4/P